Hun Pilot

Hun Pilot

Victor Vizcarra, Colonel, USAF (Ret)

THUD PILOT PRODUCTIONS
2017

Copyright © 2017 by Victor Vizcarra

All rights reserved. This book or any portion thereof may not be reproduced or used in any manner whatsoever without the express written permission of the publisher except for the use of brief quotations in a book review or scholarly journal.

First Printing: 2017

ISBN 9781973597520

Thud Pilot Productions

Dedication

Dedicated to Pat Vizcarra, my soul mate, best friend, and wife of 59 years, who supported me in my twenty-four plus years of military flying and supported me again as I relived it writing this book. I know it was much harder and more stressful the second time around! Love is forever.

V.V.

'For once you have tasted flight you will walk the earth with your eyes turned skywards, for there you have been and there you will long to return.'

- Leonardo da Vinci

Contents

Acknowledgement………………………………….……..viii

Foreword…………………………………………………... x

Preface ……………………………………………….…xiv

Introroduction……………………………………………..1

Chapter 1: Taming the Beast……………………..19

Chapter 2: Survival Training……………………..36

Chapter 3: Reporting to the Donald Duck Squadron…...45

Chapter 4: Donald Duck Becomes a Night Owl…………62

Chapter 5: Edwards Air Force Flight Test Center……...72

Chapter 6: Hun Combat ……………………………………82

Chapter 7: Academy Award Performance…………….101

Chapter 8: The Loss of "Thunder Chicken"………..108

Chapter 9: Saying Goodbye to the Hun……………...116

Chapter 10: "Sing it Again Sam"………………………124

Epilogue……………………………………………...137

Appendix……………………………………………….140

Bibliography……………………………………………146

Acknowledgement

I was pleasantly surprised and honored by all the complimentary and kind words from the readers of my first book "Thud Pilot". Your inquiries of when I would write a second book encouraged and motivated me to attempt a second manuscript.

When I started my second project, I began writing about the "Vizcarra Flying Dynasty" as my two sons like to refer to my brother's, mine, and their flying experiences which encompassed two and a half generations of Vizcarra military flying totaling close to eighty combined years. I quickly realized how much of a monumental effort this was going to be.

I want to thank and acknowledge Rory Pennington, a good friend from social media, who gave me the idea to author this book instead when he asked me when I was going to write "Hun Pilot". His question moved me to create "Hun Pilot" about my experiences flying the F-100 Super Sabre as a companion sequel to my first book, "Thud Pilot".

Computers and I just don't get along. My immediate family had to put up with a lot of frustration as I worked bringing my thoughts to paper using the computer. Pat, my wife and best friend of 59 years, took the brunt of this frustration but still had the patience to calm me when the computer would do its own thing and imitate HAL, the computer in *2001: A Space Odyssey*. She made sure I kept to and met myself imposed publishing date by threatening with a smile to not make dinner unless I wrote at least two pages a day. She kept her word and I missed dinner on a couple of occasions when I had writers block and could not even write one creative paragraph!

It goes without saying, I must also acknowledge my oldest son, Mark, for his creativity in designing the dust cover for the book. In spite of a very busy schedule writing, producing, and directing several short films, he also stayed on top of my progress with regular calls asking where I was on the book and suggesting some additional content.

His brother, Michael, equally busy playing in three professional Rock Bands, took time to not only proofread the manuscript but greatly improved it with suggested rewrites which I incorporated.

Mary, my daughter, with as busy schedule as her brother's, still took time to call each day and added to her mother's calming atmosphere. As her brothers have pointed out, she so loves the family and her calls were equally effective.

Next to the actual writing, I've found accurate proofreading is extremely difficult. I am still finding errors in "Thud Pilot" ten months and nine versions later. I've found multiple proofreaders are really required to end up with a good clean manuscript. When I think I'm done with the proofreading phase, I turn to my good friend Charles Gayre and have him have the last look, as he has the keen ability to find "hidden" errors missed by others that I really appreciate and acknowledge.

It's only appropriate to introduce a book about the Hun with a Foreword by a 2,000 plus hour F-100 Super Sabre driver and friend. Bob Terbet, from my initial operational squadron, the 309th Tactical Fighter Squadron, was kind enough to provide an interesting personal account of his flameout and successful dead stick landing as part of his Foreword.

I thank George Gifford and Jerry Stamps, close friends and fellow F-100 classmates, who were most helpful in reminding me of details of our training at Luke AFB and Nellis AFB. Without their aid, many of the training details would have been lacking in Chapter 1.

A huge thanks to Frank Castner and Al Dempsey, docents at the Palm Springs Air Museum, who retrieved specific details I requested from the museum's archives for Chapter 9. The information they provided made it possible for me to write an accurate account of Major General Kenneth P Miles' heroic mission described in the chapter.

Sam Morgan, a great friend I've known since the early 60's, had an interesting adventurous flying career full of unique experiences. I thank him for his contributions to this book, which make up Chapter 10. There are insufficient superlatives to describe his tales of humor and daring exploits.

To all my social media friends, followers, and readers, too many to acknowledge individually, you know who you are and I appreciate your encouragement; you are as responsible as the individuals mentioned above for the creation of "Hun Pilot". I thank you all.

Foreword

Vic and I first met in early 1962 as members of the 309th Tactical Fighter Squadron flying the F-100 at Homestead AFB, Florida. A little over a year later, we went our separate ways as Vic transitioned into the F-105 community. Years later, we reconnected and renewed our friendship at an Air Force reunion and have remained close friends ever since even though we only get to see each other from time to time at other reunions. My wife Ida and I enjoy these visits with Vic and Pat, picking up where we left off like it was just yesterday since we had last seen each other.

In his first book, *Thud Pilot*, Vic offered a riveting account of his combat flying experiences in Southeast Asia. The F-105 Thunderchief, known as the Thud, was the workhorse for air-to-ground missions over North Vietnam and Laos.

Vic asked me to write the foreword to this book, claiming I was the only high time Hun driver he knew. As well as his experience in the Thud, I'm sure he has enough Hun experience to more than adequately provide the reader with a thorough understanding of the Super Sabre's history and its flight characteristics.

Other than the growing pains experienced by all new aircraft, the Hun proved to be a very demanding plane to fly; especially at lower air speeds and high angles of attack. It had a Ram Air Turbine (RAT) that activated whenever the engine rpm decreased through 40 percent. This small turbine powered the hydraulic flight controls in the event of an engine flame out or failure.

On 22 March 1962, I was leading a flight of four on an air-to-air gunnery training mission just south of Death Valley, California. During the preflight briefing, I mentioned that if anyone had a dire emergency, Bicycle Lake, a dry lakebed twenty miles south used by the Army, was a divert possibility. It had a 9,000-foot runway outlined with oil and was an emergency landing site for the X-15 which was flown out of nearby Edwards AFB.

As I completed my last pass at the dart target, my engine flamed out. I was at 28,000 feet indicating 350-kts. When I announced I had flamed out, number 3 radioed, "Remember Bicycle Lake." The 335-gallon external tanks had just emptied putting the aircraft weight at approximately 30,000 lbs. I jettisoned the tanks, reduced to best glide speed of 220-kts and turned south towards Bicycle Lake. While descending, I attempted several air starts with no results.

Bicycle Lake was at 2,200-foot elevation in mountainous terrain putting the high key for the flame out pattern at 12,000 feet or so. Next, I needed three green lights on the landing gear. The main wheels free fall to a down and locked position while the nose gear is blown down using an emergency lowering procedure. My next check point was at the 7,000 foot low key abeam the lakebed followed by the base to final turn, the last opportunity to eject or commit to landing.

On final, assured I could make it to the lakebed, I lowered the flaps and with this configuration, the nose tucked. When I applied backpressure on the stick, there was no change in pitch for a second, which got my attention; rat pressure output had reduced resulting in slow control response. The touchdown was good as well as the drag chute.

Rolling out, I noticed an old red fire truck next to me. I opened the canopy and tried to stand up; I then realized that I hadn't unstrapped. When I did stand up, my legs were shaking. A jeep pulled up with two Army officers who took me to their club and bought me a beer.

There was no damage to the plane. The next day or so, a new engine was flown in from George AFB, the plane partially defueled, and was flown off the lakebed.

The flame out was caused by failure of the engine driven fuel pump, which provides fuel pressure to the normal and emergency systems.

The Hun's number was 013; North American's use of that number is questionable! A few weeks later, 013 was on a cross country to England AFB in Louisiana. On take-off at England AFB, the engine failed and the pilot ejected safely.

Prior to the war in Vietnam, from the late 1950's to 1965, the Hun was deployed worldwide and maintained a nuclear alert posture. Our 309th 1962 deployment took Vic and me to Kadena AB, Okinawa, where our squadron assumed the nuclear strike force previously assigned to the Okinawa F-100 squadrons that were transitioning to the F-105. During this deployment, then 1st Lieutenant Vizcarra, an artist as well as a fighter pilot, painted a beautiful Hun for me with 013 on its side. It hangs on a wall in our home in North Carolina, along with a portrait he did of me that he sent some 60 years later.

German born Edgar Schmued, who later became a US citizen, was an aircraft designer for North American Aviation. He was the primary designer of the P-51 Mustang, the F-86 Sabre, the F-100 Super Sabre and later at Northrop, the T-38/F-5; quite a list of classic fighters. I feel very fortunate to have flown four of the five; too young for the Mustang but 2,000 plus hours in the Hun!

Robert Terbet,
F-100 Super Sabre pilot

(Bob Terbet Photo)
Bob Terbet's Office Wall: Author's Portrait of Bob and the F-100 He Dead Stick on Bicycle Lake After Flame Out.

(Bob Terbet Photo)
Close Up of Bob Terbet Pastel Portrait

(USAF Photo)

Robert Terbet Jr. entered the Air Force through the Aviation Cadet Program in March 1956 and flew the T-34 and T-28 in Primary and the T-33 in Basic Flight training. As a Distinguished Graduate in flight training, he received a regular commission and a coveted fighter assignment. He flew the F-86F in gunnery training at Williams AFB and the F-100A in Advanced gunnery at Nellis AFB Nevada. His first operational assignment was to the 72nd and 510th TFS at Clark AB, Philippines, 1958 through 1960, followed by an assignment to the 309th TFS, 31st TFW at George AFB, California and Homestead AFB, Florida. While assigned to the 309th, he made numerous deployments to Taiwan, Italy, Germany, Okinawa, Japan, and Turkey. In 1965, he volunteered for the Skoshi Tiger program evaluating the Northrop F-5 in combat in Vietnam. At the conclusion of this assignment, he resigned from the Air Force and completed his flying career with American Airlines.

Preface

I consider myself very fortunate to have flown in what I considered the tail end of the golden age of relative early jets. An era where there was still a requirement to fly by the seat of your pants to survive. A time when the pilot, not a computer, compensated for the aerodynamic idiosyncrasies of the new era of swept wing flight. A period where throttle manipulation still necessitated a certain amount of finesse in order to not over temp the engine. A time when being a fighter pilot still meant having to acquire your adversary with your eyeballs, and maneuver in a three dimensional sphere to achieve a six o'clock kill position. Yes, it would have been fun to fly the third and fourth generation fighters, but I wouldn't have traded my experience flying the F-100 for the world.

Many of my stories in this book are of my experiences "screwing up" which may make the reader wonder how I ever survived flying the "Hun". Every aviator makes mistakes in his maturation process becoming an experienced "old" pilot. He can only become an "old" pilot by quickly learning from mistakes, his own and those of other pilots. These errors by far make much more interesting stories than normal or perfect flights. A book of perfect flights would be mundane and boring; so enjoy and take heart in my more exciting times flying the F-100 "Slick and Shiny Slightly Super Sonic Super Sabre"!

Introduction

In November 1950, the Mikoyan-Gurevich MiG-15 made its first appearance over the North Korean skies, quickly out classing the F-80C, F-84E, and all other jets operating under the United Nations flag. The USAF responded immediately and deployed three squadrons of North American Aviation (NAA) F-86A's Sabre jets, their newest fighter, to Suwon and Kimpo Air Bases in South Korea. It shouldn't have been a surprise that the world's first two swept wing fighters were so similar, they had both been designed based on German swept wing aeronautical data captured by US and Soviet forces at the end of World War II. Still, the US was surprised and impressed by the MiG's acceleration, climb and ceiling advantage over the F-86. By early 1951, NAA had improved the original F-86A, replacing the "A" production line with the "E". At the same time, the company submitted to the Air Force, an unsolicited proposal for the "Sabre 45," a much-improved new supersonic fighter design with a 45-degree wing sweep. The USAF was sufficiently impressed and interested in the proposal and inspected a full-scale mock-up at the Los Angeles North American facility in July 1951. After making over a hundred modifications requested by the Air Force, the design was accepted and assigned the designation of F-100 at the end of November of the same year.

Two YF-100A prototypes were ordered in January 1952, the first of which took to the air seventeen months later on 25 May 1953. It exceeded the sound barrier on its first flight attaining Mach 1.04. Early prototype flights achieved and demonstrated superior performance over any fighter in the USAF operational inventory.

The increasing possibility of a confrontation between the West and the Soviet block set the stage for accelerating the program and the Air Force accepted North American's proposal for early production congruent with operational test and evaluation. The first production F-100A came off the manufacturing line on 9 October 1953, a month prior to a list of design deficiencies were identified in test program reports. The most serious deficiency was yaw instability in certain flight regimes that produced a new phenomenon called inertia coupling. Increasing fineness ratios of new jet aircraft fuselages and decreasing wing spans and empennages produced inertial coupling that could result in violent pitch and yaw divergence about all three axis when the aircraft was rolled rapidly. The uncontrolled maneuver could overstress and tear an aircraft apart as was the case in the death of George Welch, North American's Chief test pilot during a test of one of the first production F-100A's.

Furthermore, the production F-100A introduced a smaller vertical tail than the two prototypes in an effort to reduce weight and drag. The design change further aggravated the yaw instability problem and was debated among a divided group of company aeronautical engineers, one group opposed to and the other in support of the change.

(USAF Photo)

Left: F-100A with Larger Vertical Tail Retrofitted to All "Short Tail" F-100A's. Right: F-100A with Smaller Vertical Tail Introduced on Initial Production Birds.

The 479th Fighter Wing, George AFB, California, became the first F-100A equipped Wing in September 1954. However, six weeks after receiving their seventieth "short tailed" F-100A, and before the Wing had achieved operational status, the Air Force grounded all F-100's due to the loss of six F-100A's in operational and test flight accidents, many of which were related to flight instability problems. The grounding remained in effect until February 1955 and the 479th did not become fully operational until September 1955. The "short tailed" F-100A's were retrofitted with new larger tails similar in size to the original prototypes' in an attempt to resolve the lateral instability problem.

The larger tails improved the lateral stability, especially at lower speeds. However, the aircraft still possessed some abnormal flight characteristics that required pilots to adapt to flying the F-100 differently than other aircraft. At high angles of attack, 200Kts and below, the F-100 became purely a rudder aircraft for turning and rolling. If aileron was applied like a conventional aircraft to turn or roll, the up aileron would be blanked out by the swept wing at high angle of attack, causing asymmetrical drag with the unblocked down aileron on the opposite wing. This would induce an adverse yawing moment causing the aircraft to turn and roll in the opposite direction of the intended flight control inputs and enter an uncoordinated tumbling maneuver about its axis similar to, but not as violent, as inertial coupling. It definitely was a flight regime to be avoided.

The F-100 was powered by the Pratt and Whitney J-57, the most powerful and advanced turbojet engine of its time. It was rated at 10,000 pounds of thrust dry (non-afterburning) and 16,000 pounds when augmented with afterburner. As advanced as it was for its day, the relative low thrust to weight ratio and throttle response time presented another challenge to pilots learning to fly the F-100. The relative long intake design did not perfectly match engine airflow requirements at low speeds and high angles of attack, causing compressor stalls if the throttle was advanced too rapidly. With the need to avoid advancing the throttle too fast, it was easy to get behind the "power curve" of the engine at the most critical phases of take-off and the landing. It was possible to get into a nose high and airspeed condition in which no amount of engine thrust was sufficient to arrest a descent rate.

The most infamous example of this occurred to Lt Barty Brooks whose assignment was to pick up and deliver aircraft to new assignment locations. Ferry pilots were constantly on the road delivering aircraft. Since the Lieutenant was a bachelor, he volunteered to be on the delivery schedule during the Christmas and New Year's holidays so a married pilot in his unit could spend the holidays at home with his family. On 10 January 1956, Lt Brooks, an experienced F-84 and F-86 pilot but with only forty hours of F-100 time, along with two other ferry pilots, picked up three new F-100C's at the North American Palmdale, California production facility for delivery to George AFB just down the road. Upon arrival at George in the landing pattern, Brook lowered his landing gear and was immediately informed by one of the other pilots, that his nose wheel scissors was disconnected from its strut and was swiveling freely. They decided to divert to Edwards AFB, California, and use its much longer runway as a precaution. Brooks requested Edwards foam an area of the runway on which to put the nose gear down. It is surmised that as Brooks approached the landing spot, he thought he was going to touch down short of the foamed area and raised the nose to extend his approach. The aircraft continued descending

The Sabre Dance
(Frames From Infamous Film)

Pilot Misjudges Touch Down Point, Starts Raising Nose to Arrest Descent.

Nose Continues to Rise, Pilot Gets Behind the Power Curve and Goes Into Afterburner.

Out of Control, Hun Stalls

Un-survivable Crash

towards touch down and Brooks continued pulling the nose up trying to break the descent. He was late in adding power and the wings started stalling at the wing tips. The decreasing lift over the stalling wing continued to progress towards the wing root, shifting the aircraft's center of gravity aft and forcing the nose even higher. By now, Brooks had advanced the throttle to full military power, but it was too late, he was behind the power curve. The wings started rocking side-to-side, as Brook went into afterburner, the engine compressor stalled and the aircraft yawed right perpendicular to the runway. He was no longer in control of the F-100C as the aircraft was now close to a ninety degree bank with the right wing less than ten feet above the ground. The right wing struck the ground and the aircraft went tumbling in a huge fireball just off the left edge of the runway, killing the Lieutenant. An Edwards camera test crew near the runway captured the accident on film and it became known as the "Sabre Dance". It was the most viewed movie of an F-100 behind the power curve, shown to all F-100 student pilots before they ever took their first flight in a Super Sabre. Unfortunately, it would not be the last "Sabre Dance".

The F-100A was designed as an air superiority day fighter in the lineage of its predecessor, the North American F-86. The aircraft provided the Air Force a truly supersonic fighter with greater performance than anything else in its or the Navy's inventory.

NAA's first supersonic design benefited from the ever-increasing 1950's tension between the West and the Soviet Block. The Air Force recognized they had a potential jewel with the speed of the F-100 and requested six airframes be modified for the photoreconnaissance mission in a highly secretive program named *Slick Chick*. The aircraft were extensively modified, the four M-39 guns and associated ammo cans were removed and much of the electrical components were relocated aft of the cockpit to make room for installation of five high resolution aerial survey cameras in the lower nose. The vacated area was deepened giving the aircraft a distinctive look making it impossible to hide the aircraft's reconnaissance mission and pass as a standard F-100.

An additional 830 gallon fuel tank was added internally along with two extra 200 gallon wing tanks, allowing up to five and a half hour missions.

Designated RF-100A's, they provided early high altitude, supersonic photographic intrusions over Soviet Block territory in Eastern Europe. Initially, three of the RF-100A's were assigned to USAFE, the other three were sent to PACAF for operations in the Far East. The program was extremely successful, especially in Europe, with over eight hundred missions being flown between 1955 and 1958, many of which were over Soviet controlled Eastern Europe. These missions provided the first photographic evidence of European Soviet missile installations.

Two RF-100A's were lost in operational accidents. The four remaining examples were transferred to the Republic of China Air Force in 1958 where they operated through 1960.

(Stock Photo)

Slick Chick **Program RF-100A Photoreconnaissance Airframe**

As superior as the F-100A was, it had one of the highest accident rates in the Air Force inventory. This along with changing mission requirements resulted in an Air Force Request For Proposal (RFP) for an improved fighter-bomber version capable of delivering a tactical nuclear bomb.

The new fighter-bomber version was designated the F-100C; the F-100B being a short lived designation of a radically redesigned F-100 in response to an entirely different Request for Proposal (RFP) for a low level, high speed, all weather tactical nuclear fighter-bomber. The F-100B was quickly re-designated the YF-107A, more accurately reflecting the totally new design in response to the RFP.

(Stock Picture)

Originally Designated F-100B, It Was Determined Sufficiently Different and Redesignated the YF-107A. The Design Lost to the F-105 in a Competitive Test Program and Never Entered Production.

(Stock Photo)

F-100A Modified as "C" Prototype Demonstrating Fighter-Bomber Configuration.

The major improvements incorporated in the F-100C which first entered service in July 1955 were an up-rated J57-P-21 engine, a "wet" wing (internal wing fuel tanks versus the F-100A dry wing), mid-air refueling capability, yaw and pitch dampers to improve flight stability, increased external stores to seven stations, three on each wing, and a centerline fuselage station, and a Low Altitude Bombing System (LABS) for over the shoulder nuclear weapon delivery. These changes transitioned the F-100 to a totally new mission from air superiority to primarily tactical ground attack while retaining an air-to-air capability. However, with the exceptions of the yaw and pitch dampers, these changes did little to address the design deficiencies plaguing the F-100 from the on-set and the high accident rate continued with 85 "C" models lost in major accidents over its 15 year career.

At the same time the F-100C was coming on the scene, the US Navy was in the midst of developing the "Sidewinder" self-guiding air-to-air missile. Glenn Tierney, a young pilot who had started his naval career during World War II was in charge of the Sidewinder Testing and Development Project being conducted at the Naval Ordnance Test Station (NOTS) at China Lake, California. The missile's test performance was exceeding expectations such that the developers sought to expand the missile's capabilities to include shooting down a high-flying supersonic target. Navy LCDR. Tierney's calculations supported this expanded capability as long as the launching platform was supersonic. This presented a dilemma to the Navy program as Naval Aviation did not yet possess an operational supersonic fighter in its inventory.

The Air Force had taken interest in the missile's development and assigned a General Officer to the program who provided an F-100 for the supersonic test. Nellis expected Tierney to go through a short two-week checkout program but Tierney's test schedule only allowed time for one day of ground school, followed by a single check out flight the following day. After the single Hun flight at Nellis, Tierney returned back to China Lake to continue on with other Sidewinder tests while awaiting his F-100 to come off the production line at Palmdale, California.

In preparation for the high altitude tests, Tierney was fitted for and trained in a high altitude chamber wearing a high altitude pressure flight suit and helmet.

The final week of March 1957, saw all the necessary pieces come together to conduct the high altitude supersonic tests at Holloman AFB, Alamogordo, New Mexico. A series of tests against Ryan BQM-34 Firebee target drones and Sidewinder launches against high altitude balloons at 63,000 and 80,000 feet, culminated in a test firing at a supersonic Bomarc long range surface-to-air missile. The Bomarc was more like a pilotless aircraft, at one time even being designated the F-99. Launched from a vertical position, the missile, propelled by rocket boosters to high altitude, would transition into level flight above 50,000 feet and was capable of cruising at 2.5 Mach powered by two ramjet engines. On 30 March 1957, LCDR Tierney, flying an F-100C at Mach 1.4 and 55,000 feet, became the first pilot to shoot down a supersonic target, a Bomarc flying at Mach 1.3, proving the Sidewinder's capability to destroy a high-flying supersonic target.

(USN Photos)

USN LCDR. Glenn Tierney, AIM-9 "Sidewinder" Development Chief Test Pilot, Made the First High Altitude Supersonic Target Shoot Down by an AIM-9 fired From a Supersonic F-100C at 55,000 Feet.

(Personal Photo)
Bomarc Supersonic Missile Served as Target For Supersonic Launch of an AIM-9 From an F-100C.

In mid 1954, North American began a study for a two-seat trainer version of the F-100C as a means of addressing the accident rate. In September 1955, the Air Force accepted the company's proposal to convert an F-100C to a dual seat demonstrator at no cost to the government. The aircraft, designated as a TF-100C, made its maiden flight eleven months later in August 1956. The demonstrator was short lived, crashing nine months later during spin tests. The company test pilot successfully ejected and survived the accident.

With the definitive model of the F-100 starting to enter service only a month after the crash of the prototype TF-100C, it become logical that if there was to be a two-seat trainer version of an F-100, it should be based on the latest version, the "D."

The F-100D corrected not only "C" model operational deficiencies but it finally addressed the challenging flight characteristics inherent in the design from day one. The fuselage to wing fineness ratio was decreased with the extension of the wing span by 26 inches and addition of 27% more vertical tail area. Although not entirely eliminating the inertial coupling tendency of the original F-100, these changes greatly reduced it. However, these changes had no affect on the adverse yaw characteristic and the corrective action for this undesirable flight condition was to train F-100 pilots to use only rudder for turning and rolling in the high angle of attack flight regime.

In response to the 1950's threat of nuclear war and annihilation of runways, the Air Force initiated a test program for zero-length launch (ZEL) of an F-100D configured with a nuclear weapon training shape. The concept used a 130,000 lb thrust Rocketdyne M-34 solid rocket booster to launch the F-100 from an elevated ramp on a mobile trailer.

(USAF Photo)

Early ZEL Test. F-100D Configured with Single 275 Gallon Wing Tank. Later Test Added Mk-7 Nuclear Training Shape on Opposite Wing.

The program successfully conducted twenty test launches over a fifteen-month period between 1958 and 1959, proving the feasibility of the concept. The last 148 F-100D's came off the production line with the ZEL modification, although the concept was never used operationally.

The "D" model entered service at the end of September 1956 and in addition to the increases in wing and vertical tail areas, it added trailing edge wing flaps and a totally redesigned aircraft electrical system. The constant speed drive of the new electrical system however, proved to be unreliable and a constant maintenance problem in the early service years of the "D" fleet. Eventually, it and other reliability problems were resolved by numerous and various modifications. However, these fixes created new maintenance and operational challenges of having various nonstandard configurations among the 700 individual airframes. In 1965, the fleet underwent a "High Wire" modification program, which standardized the aircraft design configuration.

(Bill Dillard Photo)
F-100D, Definitive Version of the Super Sabre.

The two-seat F-100F combat trainer was designed with the same combat capability as the single seat "D" except for two less M-39 20mm cannons and was produced simultaneously with the "Ds" last two production years in 1957 and 1958. Ironically, the introduction of operational "Fs" did nothing to reduce the high F-100 accident rate and the fleet experienced the deadliest year with the loss of 116 F-100s and 47 pilots killed in 1958.

(Dave Everson Photo)

F-100F, 80th Tac Ftr Sqdn, Circa 1962

North American offered to send Bob Hoover, their Chief Test pilot, to each F-100 base and have him demonstrate the F-100's low speed capability to boost Air Force pilots' confidence in this regime of flight in which many of the accidents were occurring. I got to witness one of these demonstrations during a 1958 air show at George AFB. Mr. Hoover walked out to the flight line and randomly picked out an F-100 that was ready for flight. On take-off, he pulled up 30 degrees and at 100 feet, slowly rudder rolled the aircraft with the landing gear and flaps still extended. As he completed the 360-degree roll, he pulled up to downwind in the landing pattern and to the surprise of the show attendees, landed immediately, making it one of the shortest demonstrations ever seen! He climbed out of the aircraft and had a short talk with the crew chief before walking over to another F-100. He took off in the second F-100 and repeated the dirty roll maneuver on take-off and proceeded to put on a full demonstration flying several slow speed maneuvers in different aircraft configurations. I later learned that he had air aborted the first flight because the airplane was not correctly rigged. It is amazing that Bob Hoover had such a feel for the 100 that he was able to detect the plane was not properly rigged in one maneuver immediately after getting airborne.

By late nineteen fifties, the F-100 had become the Air Force's mainstay fighter-bomber with nearly 2,000 aircraft assigned to Tactical Air Command, US Air Forces European Command, and Pacific Air Forces Command. Tactical Air Command F-100 units were highly mobile and began regular deployments worldwide to sit nuclear alert at bases on the periphery of the Soviet Union and Communist China.

By the time the "Winds of War" over Southeast Asia were looming in early 1960's, the F-100 and its pilots had matured as an effective weapon system, with numerous deployments to world "hot spots." In 1964, hostilities greatly intensified in Laos with the communist Pathet Lao's conquest of the Plaine des Jarres posing an increased threat to the "neutrality" of Laos arranged by the Geneva Conference in 1954. The US Navy lost two aircraft, an RF-8A on a reconnaissance flight on 6 June 1964 and a F-8 escorting another reconnaissance flight the very next day when they were shot down over the Plaine. The US responded by sending eight F-100D's from the 405th TFW at Clark AB, Philippines, TDY to Da Nang AB, RVN from which to attack the Pathet Lao.

A less than successful first F-100 combat mission of the war was flown on 9 June 1964 when eight F-100D's attempted to attack a small motor pool in a Pathet Lao stronghold in the Plaine des Jarres. The 2nd Air Division Commander altered the mission commander's well-planned strike, changing the weapons load and time of attack that placed the aircraft over the target during the day's worst weather. This higher headquarters' infringement was a harbinger of how the war in Southeast Asia would be mismanaged by the chain of command extending all the way to the White House.

On 7 August 1964, the war expanded beyond the Laotian boarders and overflowed into North Vietnam when the joint US Congress passed the Gulf of Tonkin Resolution. The resolution gave President Lyndon B. Johnson authority to use conventional military force in Southeast Asia without the declaration of war by congress.

The F-100's first fray into North Vietnam occurred on 8 February 1965, when 20 F-100's flew flak suppression in a joint mission with VNAF A-1's attacking RVN army barracks at Chap Le, 15 miles north of the Demilitarized Zone (DMZ) separating North and South Vietnam.

2 March 1965 saw the start of "Rolling Thunder," the gradual systematic bombing of North Vietnam targets designed to dissuade the North Vietnamese government from continuing its efforts to overthrow the South Vietnamese government. Forty-four F-100D's, in the defense suppression role, preceded a mixed force of F-105's and B-57's and attacked Triple-A sites protecting the Xom Bong ammo storage area with 2.75 inch rockets and 20mm cannon fire. Lieutenant Hayden Lockhart, Jr., became the first and longest serving US pilot prisoner of war (POW) in North Vietnam when his F-100D was shot down while attacking one of these Triple-A sites. He was repatriated on 12 Feb 1973, 2,905 days after his capture.

The only probable air-to-air shoot down by an F-100 occurred on 4 April 1965. Capt Don Kilgus in aircraft 55-2894 was flying a Rescue Combat Air Patrol (RESCAP) mission as number 2 in "Green" flight off the coast of North Vietnam. The flight was jumped by a pair of MiG-17s head-on. In a violent diving turning fight, Kilgus ended up at 6 o'clock to one of the MiGs and fired a series of 20mm bursts before having to break off as he passed through 7,000 feet and avoid crashing into the ocean. He and other flight members observed hits and pieces flying off the MiG still diving towards the water. His shoot-down claim was denied by the Air Force since no bailout or crash was actually witnessed; instead, he was credited with a "Probable." This official status was never changed and remained as a "Probable" even after RVNAF records obtained after the war verified that three MiG-17s were lost that day, two to friendly ground fire, and the third assumed to have been shot down by enemy (U.S.) action.

The F-100 continued flying Barrel Roll and Steal Tiger interdiction missions in Laos and flak suppression Rolling Thunder escort missions over North Vietnam for the next few months. But as the missions progressed further into North Vietnam it became more difficult for the Hun to keep up with the F-105, which had become the Air Force's main fighter-bomber for missions over the North. The F-100's Rolling Thunder missions were curtailed by mid-1965 and the Hun was relegated to interdiction and close air support duties in South Vietnam.

Although the Hun had become the USAF's mainstay fighter-bomber for South Vietnam operations, the "F" reappeared over North Vietnam skies in specialized missions. The disastrous F-105 "Spring High" 27 July 1965 attack on North Vietnamese Surface-to-Air Missile (SAM) sites revealed the need for a specialized aircraft equipped to locate, and destroy the SAM threat. Seven F-100F's quickly modified as the first "Wild Weasel" aircraft for the SAM suppression mission deployed to Korat RTAFB the latter part of Nov 1965. The first F-100F "Iron Hand," as SAM suppression missions were called, was flown 3 December 1965, and the first successful Wild Weasel "kill" of a SAM site was achieved on the 22nd of the month.

The Wild Weasel concept had been proven with nine SAM sites destroyed by spring of 1966. However, it wasn't without cost! The North Vietnamese scored first, shooting down a Wild Weasel three days before the first successful Weasel SAM kill. The mixed team of an F-100F as the hunter and the F-105's as the killers was also hampered by the same challenge that plagued the earlier F-100D fighter escort missions; it was too slow compared to the F-105. With combat losses and accidents dwindling the available numbers of F-100F Wild Weasels, the F-105F became the logical replacement as the "Wild Weasel III" (The Wild Weasel II was an unsuccessful attempt to modify the F-4C for the SAM suppression role). By May 1966, the first F-105F Wild Weasels had arrived at Korat AB and the last F-100F Weasel mission was flown in July 1966.

However, the replacement of the few remaining F-100F Wild Weasels with F-105F Wild Weasels was not the end of F-100 combat missions over North Vietnam. Another new specialized mission, the fast Forward Air Controller (FAC), had its geneses at 7th Air Force under Project Commando Sabre in mid-1966. The skies over North Vietnam had become too lethal and a new approach was needed to accomplish the Cessna O-1 "Bird Dog" and O-2 Skymaster FAC mission of interdicting enemy supply lines in Route Pack 1 (North Vietnam was divided into six Route Packs 1 through 6 for assigning responsibility between the Air Force and the Navy assets. Route Pack 1 was the southern most Pack bordering the DMZ. The other Packs covered the rest of North Vietnam in sequence with Packs 5 and 6 being the two furthest northern Packs separating North Vietnam and China. Route Pack 6 was later sub-divided into Packs 6A and 6B).

Under Project Commando Sabre, a concept emerged to employ F-100F's in the FAC role using speed for survival. Forward Air Controller trained F-100 pilots would alternate between flying the aircraft from the front seat or functioning as the FAC searching, locating, and directing the strike from the rear cockpit. This specialized group of pilots was all volunteers, who proudly operated under the

"Misty" call sign by which the program became more commonly known. "Misty" operations were sustained by 157 pilots over the life of the program from mid-1967 to mid-1970. This elite group produced a disproportionate number of highly successful alumni; Air Force Chief of Staff Generals Merrill "Tony" McPeak and Ronald Fogleman; Medal of Honor recipient, POW, and first "Misty" unit commander Colonel George E. "Bud" Day; and Dick Rutan, of around the world non-stop, un-refueled flight in the "Voyager" fame.

All Super Sabre models, except the "A," saw action in Southeast Asia. After seven years of combat, the last F-100's were withdrawn from Southeast Asia in July 1971 having flown 360,283 combat sorties, the most of any fighter.

The Hun continued to soldier on another eight years with Air National Guard units until they were totally phased out in 1979, having served a year past a quarter of a century. After retirement, 219 Super Sabres were converted to QF-100 Full Scale Aerial Target Drones. Out of the total 2,294 F-100's built, 889 were lost in accidents killing 324 pilots, and another 186 Huns were lost to enemy action in Southeast Asia.

Unlike the F-105 which none remain in flyable status, several examples of the F-100 have been preserved in flying condition. The last airworthy single seat Hun, an ex-Turkish Air Force F-100 repatriated by a US civilian, flew during the 2004 Reno Air Races and that aircraft is now displayed as the last flyable F-100D at the Palm Springs Air Museum in California. The two most notable examples still flying are the Collins Foundation F-100F painted to represent "Bud" Day's aircraft, 56-3851 (actual airframe is 56-3844) and Dean "Cutter" Cutshall's "F" aircraft 56-3948 in colorful markings of the late fifties. Fortunately, these two aircraft will provide new generations the experience to see and hear the first US supersonic fighter, designed nearly 65 years ago, takeoff with AB roaring for years to come.

(Christopher A. Ebdon Photo)

Collins Foundation F-100F in the Markings of Medal of Honor Hero "Bud" Day.

(Stock Photo)

Most Popular Civilian F-100F Owned and Flown by Dean "Cutter" Cutshall's

Chapter 1: Taming The Beast

When I reported to Luke AFB in Glendale, Arizona, 21 May 1961, I had just graduated from Air Force pilot training and had 263 hours of military flying time plus my prior 120 hours in civilian light planes. I was fortunate to graduate high enough in my class to choose the third of six F-100 assignments available. It didn't take long to realize the student atmosphere at Tactical Air Command's F-100 schoolhouse was very different from Air Training Command's attitude from which I had just come. Here, we were treated like the future fighter pilots we were to become, "everyman a Tiger." The first time I sat in an F-100 cockpit, my thought was, "Wow, it's big. I don't know if I can handle this!" That was the last questionable thought I had about the F-100. At Luke, we were trained in an atmosphere that we were the best, could do anything, and we didn't lack confidence in flying the Super Sabre. It was a wonder that our heads fit through the door by the time we graduated.

(Stock Photo)

Author's Future Office, F-100 Cockpit.

The course was front loaded with academics and the Instrument Flight Training phase. Academics covered aircraft systems, flight characteristics, local area procedures, and nuclear and conventional weapons. The infamous "Sabre Dance" movie was a major theme and was shown as part of the flight characteristic lecture.

This was a period when the two super powers were in a dangerous nuclear arms race; it was the height of the cold war and the F-100 was Tactical Air Command's primary nuclear delivery system. Our nuclear weapons training was conducted in a secured compound separated from the rest of the base by a high chain link fence topped with barbed wire. We were given access to an F-100 with a Mk-7 nuclear bomb loaded on an inboard station and were shown classified movies of nuclear bomb tests that showed the devastating affects on different structures, which now, fifty-six years later, anyone can see on YouTube. I was awe-struck by the tremendous responsibility with which I was going to be entrusted.

Finally in mid-June, we reported to the Instrument Flight Training Section for our first flights, which were not in the F-100, but the T-33 from which I had just graduated the month prior. In basic flight training, although I did okay, instrument flying was my weakest phase. In my very first flight at Luke, I busted the ride when I misread the instrument let down plate and flew the penetration turn in reverse. Luckily, the penetration was over a flat valley and the instructor pilot (IP) in the front seat did not have to take control of the aircraft to avoid any obstructing terrain. He just let me complete the flight without saying anything until we debriefed the mission. The instructor was smiling as he debriefed me and said I had actually flown good instruments with the exception of the major error. Unfortunately, it was a dangerous error and under other conditions, could have been fatal; it required a pink grade sheet indicating I had failed the ride. He tried to put me at ease by telling me not to worry about the failed ride but it certainly was not an auspicious start in a new program.

Sadly, I dwelled on my mistake, got nervous, and only did slightly better on the next flight. I didn't do anything dangerous, but my instrument cross check wasn't near as good as the previous flight. This time, the instructor's debrief wasn't as reassuring nor as encouraging and resulted in a below average grade for the flight. I felt like I was getting behind the power curve and I hadn't even gotten into an F-100 yet! I

(Stock Photo)
T-33 Lead-in Instrument Trainer for F-100 Instrument Phase.

thought I needed a new fresh start so I went to the Instrument Flight Training Section Chief and explained the situation, told him how I felt, and tactfully requested reassignment to another instructor. I was very concerned about a possible negative reaction to my request but it turned out all right and I was assigned to another instructor. The change worked and I was able to satisfactorily complete the Instrument phase.

Six weeks after arriving at Luke AFB for the twenty-six week F-100 training course, we finally reported to our F-100 flight class. Our class was split between two different flights; I, along with ten other students, was assigned to "Little Joe" Reynolds' flight. "Little Joe" was given this handle because of his size; he could have been a football linebacker! A terrific leader, he had confidence in himself, the F-100, and his students. He epitomized the "everyman a tiger" attitude in which he had flourished as a fighter pilot. We were not tied to a specific instructor, flying with all instructors in "Little Joe's" flight.

On 10 July, I had my first F-100F transition flight. I flew similar missions the next four consecutive days and then two more the following Monday. The air work consisted of getting the feel for the aircraft by doing basic aircraft maneuvers including high angle of attack rolls using only the rudder and practicing simulated landing patterns at altitude. Returning to the field, we did multiple touch and go landings plus simulated flame out approaches. The next day, with seven sorties, seven hours and forty minutes, and eighteen landings experience in the "F", I had my first solo flight in an F-100C.

I was surprised that the first solo was totally unsupervised and not chased by an IP. We were given a tail number to go to on the ramp, did our preflight, start up and taxi like we knew what we were doing. We were told to practice a lot of rudder rolls in our air work. They wanted us to get used to using a lot of rudder flying the F-100. I flew two more "C" flights the very next day. It felt so good to fly a fighter by yourself. At this early stage, I certainly wasn't a fighter pilot yet, but I sure felt like a "Tiger."

After that very brief period of flying non-tethered to an IP, we found ourselves back in the F-100F to start the formation-flying phase. Each student flew at least one "F" formation sortie with an IP and then was cleared to "C's.

Each phase brought new experiences, thrills, and appreciation for the airplane. I was amazed by the faith and confidence "Little Joe" had in his students. After several formation flights and with less then 20 hours in the Hun, "Little Joe" leading a formation flight of three solo students, put us in extended trail (aircraft lined up behind each other with one airplane spacing between aircraft) and dove into a loop. As he was going over the top of the loop inverted, he radioed, "Everybody, check your airspeed." I was surprised he was telling students to momentarily shift their concentration from the aircraft in front of them to the airspeed indicator in the cockpit. Each aircraft trailing behind lead was still approaching the apex of the loop, and as I checked my airspeed, I was simultaneously surprised and impressed to see the airspeed needle passing through 80-kts towards zero! In the flight debriefing, it become obvious "Little Joe" was showing us the stability of the aircraft and that as long as the ailerons were neutral, it could be controlled below landing speeds.

This demonstration further increased our growing confidence in the F-100 and ourselves. The training program included "buddy flights" where students were scheduled in a pair of "C's to go fly without an instructor. George Gifford, a good friend and classmate, and I got to share one of these flights. We took turns flying as lead and as wingman. When Gifford took the lead, he signaled me to go trail and once he saw I was in position in his mirrors, he dove to build up his airspeed and smoothly pulled up into the vertical. He held us going straight up until as he said, "We were out of airspeed and ideas" as we fell out of the sky. When he checked his mirrors again, he was surprised to see I was still in position!

As our confidence grew, our training class experienced its first disastrous accident reminding us of the reality that the F-100 could jump up and bite you. Leading a formation take-off, a student in the front cockpit of an "F", failed to compensate for the slightly higher thrust of the "F" and didn't reduce his power a couple percent to equalize his student wingman's power in the "C". The "F" quickly out accelerated the "C" and Pete Hassel, the solo student from our sister flight, attempted to rotate with Lead but didn't have the necessary speed to get safely airborne. The "C" staggered into the air but started to settle back down as it climbed out of ground effect. Pete instinctively applied more backpressure raising the nose further and quickly got behind the power curve. He flew down the runway, nose high, the wings rocking side to side reminiscent of the feared "Sabre Dance." The only thing that could possibly have saved him would have been for someone to call him to lower his nose. But that call never came and he crashed in a farmer's field right outside the field boundaries and was killed.

Pete's loss was not the only accident our class experienced. Lt. Col. Bruno Grabowsky, Commander of the 104th Tactical Fighter Group (TFG), Massachusetts Air National Guard (ANG) and ranking student in our class, was leading George Gifford on a formation take-off when Grabowsky's "C" caught fire. George radioed Bruno he was on fire and to turn right towards the White Mountains. Instead, Grabowsky started turning left towards Phoenix but the controls froze almost immediately and the Colonel ejected when the F-100 started nosing over. Later, when George asked him why he didn't follow his call to turn towards the White Mountains, Grabowsky in his typical gruff manner, answered, "I don't believe Lieutenants."

Fourteen years later, now Lt. Col. George Gifford reported to the 104th TFG as the Air Force Advisor to the Guard. He wondered if Grabowsky was still around or retired, and if so, hopefully still living in the area so he could look him up. When he entered the Group Headquarters, he was surprised to find Colonel Grabowsky sitting behind the Group Commander's desk and was greeted with, "I don't believe Lt. Colonels either!" For the next four years, George and the Colonel, the oldest F-100 pilot in the unit, had a great and enjoyable working relationship.

A third accident during our time at Luke demonstrated that experience in the aircraft didn't make one immune to accidents. An instructor pilot returning from a weekend cross-country flew into the ground and was killed while doing a night TACAN penetration and approach to the field; maybe it was flying that was intrinsically dangerous and not the F-100!

Finally, we entered the phase of training that would make us fighter pilots - weapons delivery. Our training was heavily weighted towards nuclear weapons due to the Cold War tension between the Soviet Union, Red China, and the West. I estimate close to eighty percent of the weapons training syllabus dealt with nuclear delivery. But conventional skip bombing was what got my attention the most. I'll never forget being in the front seat as Capt. Hunt, the IP, flying from the rear seat, made a diving base turn to 50 feet, lined up on final run-in towards the skip bomb box with the target banner stretched across it, and expertly got a skip hit without even the advantage of a bomb sight; I was impressed! I had already flown fairly low and fast during the nuclear delivery phase that preceded conventional weapons training, but Capt. Hunt's skip bomb demonstration was my first experience flying that close to the ground that fast!

Nuclear deliveries involved low altitude approaches to the target. The F-100's Low Altitude Bombing System (LABS) was one of the earliest delivery methods created after World War II and was initially developed for the Boeing B-47. The LABS provided the delivery aircraft the time needed to escape the nuclear blast by flinging the bomb thousands of feet high; more than doubling the bomb time of flight before impact and detonation.

LABS deliveries were commonly called "Over the Shoulder" bombing as under certain conditions; the bomb could be released past the vertical portion of the delivery maneuver. We approached the target at 200 feet and 500-kts with the LABS switches previously set. At the target, we depressed and held the pickle button (bomb release) and commenced a four "G" Immelmann or half Cuban Eight delivery maneuver. Flying to center the vertical and horizontal needles on the "Dive and Roll" instrument gauge assured a wings level four "G" maneuver. A bomb release light illuminated when the LABS automatically released the weapon at a predetermined angle manually set on the system vertical gyro before flight. On the gunnery range, we would complete the delivery using an Immelmann since we would remain in the gunnery pattern doing multiple deliveries. In actual combat, we would have flown a half Cuban Eight to accelerate faster in a dive towards the deck to achieve maximum separation.

The LABS vertical gyro was located underneath the saddleback, a panel on the top of the aircraft behind the canopy that had to be removed for the pilot to set the gyro as part of his preflight. A dentist mirror was needed to read and set the scaled dial on the gyro. This setting was crucial for accuracy when dropping an actual nuclear bomb or full size training shape. After being shown how to set the gyro on our first LABS mission, we never had to set the gyro again in training; we just used the same setting on our daily training. We flew a lot of "Over the Shoulder" missions and got proficient at easily achieving bomb scores within the 1,350-foot qualification criteria.

The LABS system also had a pair of timers for Low Altitude Drogue Delivery (LADD). This allowed us to deliver a drogue chute equipped nuclear weapon at lower angles than the near vertical over the shoulder LABS toss method. LADD was based on time rather than LABS pitch angle and was more accurate by almost 40 percent. We approached the target at 1,000 feet and Mach 0.7 (460-kts). At a previously selected point designated as the Initial Point (IP), some distance from the target, the pickle button was depressed and held to start the LABS pull up timer. We'd start a 4G pull when the "Pull Up" light illuminated at the expiration of the timer. The second LADD timer began its timing sequence with the "Pull Up" signal and released the weapon at termination of its time. The bomb released at a much lower angle than in the over the shoulder deliveries and the drogue chute provided the safe separation between bomb detonation and the escaping delivery aircraft. At bomb release, we'd roll inverted, pull down, and roll upright at low altitude for escape. An 800-foot or less hit within the target was a qualifying bomb.

Depending on the type of bomb, nuclear weapons deliveries were flown low altitude between 200 and 1,000 feet, culminating in a climbing delivery maneuver. Conventional weapons delivery was just the opposite. It involved starting a dive from a higher altitude and hurling yourself at the ground! To paraphrase Douglas Adams, a noted author and satirist, the knack to flying lies in learning how to throw yourself at the ground and miss! Because of this, I found conventional weapon delivery more fun, exciting, and challenging.

Before flying our first air-to-ground rocket delivery mission, we were shown gun camera film recovered from an F-84F student who crashed while firing rockets. The purpose of showing us the film was to emphasize that the margin for error is very small during rocket delivery and if you watched your rockets hit the ground, you were probably going to be next at 12 o'clock! With the rocket firing parameters of 400-kts, 30-degree dive and 2,500 release altitude, you are only 7.5 seconds away from hitting the ground. I found achieving a rocket circular error average (CEA) of 90 feet needed to qualify a little more challenging than the 140 foot CEA 45-degree dive bombing qualification criteria.

The challenge in dive-bombing was learning the correct roll-in technique relative to the target so the pipper and the point you are aiming for were reached simultaneously at the release altitude. If you did not start with a good roll-in, you'd be playing catch up ball and most likely would not be able to achieve all necessary parameters simultaneously. Bombing can be accomplished at 45, 30, and 15-degree dive angles but at Luke we were only instructed in the 45-degree dive. Once you learned the basics of dive-bombing, it was easy to adapt to low angle dive-bombing later at your operational base.

Skip bombing entailed flying a final approach at 50 feet and 400-kts towards the target, a relative easy task. As easy as it was, it was critical to be in level flight when the bombsight intersected the target. An ever

(Stock Photo)

F-100C Flying 50 Foot Skip Bomb Approach.

so slight climb produced an early sight picture resulting in an early bomb release short of the target. Similarly, a slight descending attitude produced a late sight picture resulting in a late release and a long bomb. Still, skip bombing was easy and a lot of fun in a training environment; it was not a good attack tactic in actual combat. Skip bombing qualification required getting a minimum of 50% hits on the vertical banner stretched across the center of a 50 by 200 foot outlined area called the skip box.

The last event we'd fly on a conventional weapons training mission was strafe. The gun limiter would be set for 100 rounds and you had to get at least 25% hits against a 20 x 20 foot strafe target to qualify. We'd strafe in a 5 to 8 degree dive at 400-kts, firing between 2,000 and 1,500 feet slant range. The targets were set 600 feet behind a cease-fire foul line. The most dangerous aspects of strafe were picking up ricochets if you pressed in too close or had a low pull out. Later in my career, functioning as a range officer, I've seen the 20 x 20 foot banners ripped apart by the wing vortices from a low pull out. Similarly to rockets, the margin for error in strafe was very small.

Author's "Hero Picture" at Conclusion of F-100 Training Course, Luke AFB, Arizona, Nov 1961

(Personal Photo)

On 29 Nov 1961, I completed the 26 week F-100 Fighter Course and graduated as a fighter pilot with 108 hours in the F-100C/F. Now it was time to attend what was equivalent to post graduate F-100 school. But before reporting to Nellis AFB, Las Vegas, Nevada, for Advanced F-100 gunnery school, I had to attend Air Force Survival School at Stead AFB, near Reno, Nevada.

Upon graduation from Pilot Training, those of us who chose F-100 assignments also had a choice of when to attend survival school. Anxious to start flying the F-100, I chose to attend survival school between the two F-100 gunnery-training courses, not a good decision! Who would elect to go through survival training in the Sierra Nevada mountain range in the dead of winter? Obviously, someone too anxious to get into F-100 training to really analyze the situation! You'll read the results of this miscalculation in the next chapter.

I reported to Nellis on 2 Jan 1962, after withstanding the tribulations of survival school and being converted from a city slicker to one who might be able to actually survive in the wilderness long enough to be rescued. At Nellis, we would be taught mid-air refueling, air-to-air gunnery, low-level tactical navigation, and attacking simulated targets on an uncontrolled tactical range (vehicle convoys, gun emplacements, and airfields).

Typical of other training programs, before we started flying we had classroom orientation with briefings on local procedures, the Nellis Military Operating Area (MOA), emergency recovery fields, etc. One thing that stood out and got our curiosity was the briefing on the MOA containing Groom Lake that later became known as the infamous Area 51. The runway at Groom Lake was listed as one of our emergency recover airfields. The briefer emphasized that while flying in this MOA, if we happened to come upon, his words, "a strange looking flying object," we were to turn away and continue on with our mission in another portion of the MOA without calling out the object. He continued on and in very certain terms, instructed us to not speak to anyone, even within our own flight members, of what we had seen. Of course the first thing that came to our minds, at least mine, was UFO's!

Prior to my first flight, which was going to be air refueling, I went to Personal Equipment to trade in my worn out flight gloves for new ones. Unfortunately, they were out of my size and I had no choice but to accept the next size larger as my old ones were so badly worn. I didn't like the feel of the excess material at the ends of the fingers in the new gloves and had to pull the gloves real tight to fill the empty space at the ends of the fingers as much as possible. Although, the gloves felt very uncomfortable, I didn't think it would affect my flying ability.

Still very young, new, and inexperienced, I was easily impressed by the experience of the instructors, especially when my instructor turned out to be a First Lieutenant who didn't look much older than myself. Upon meeting him, I wondered how he had accumulated enough experience to be an instructor in the F-100. After Lead briefed the flight, we walked out to our airplanes; we were flying as number two.

It had been 41 days since my last flight. I was anxious to get back in the air, not nervous and more confident than I should have been for the amount of hours I had in the F-100. With my trusty Lieutenant instructor in the back seat of the "F", I completed my after engine start checks like I was an experienced F-100 pilot, and was ready to taxi when the flight lead called for taxi. Taxi out, and take-off were normal and I was set on doing an impressive straight ahead join-up with lead.

After getting airborne, I stayed in burner until I reached a 50-kt overtake. Passing through 2,000 feet, I disconnected my zero lanyard from my parachute "D" ring and started to stow it on its little wire ring on my parachute harness (For ejections below 2,000 feet, the lanyard should be connected to the "D" ring for quicker opening chute; above 2,000 feet, it should be disconnected for a delayed opening to increase man seat separation). As I was attempting to stow the lanyard, I realized I was fast approaching the join up and needed to reduce the power. I let go of the lanyard to reach for the throttle and the damn lanyard clasp accidentally hooked on to the excess webbing between my thumb and index finger of my oversized glove! When my hand reached the throttle, I felt the resistance of the lanyard as it reached its maximum extension. This was followed by the ticking noise of the parachute timer and then I felt the pilot chute pop out and push me forward on the seat.

I couldn't worry about what was going on with my parachute; I had to concentrate on completing the join-up on lead. Once I completed the join-up and had everything under control, I told my IP I thought I had just popped my chute. I was looking at him in the review mirrors to see his reaction and could see him checking the rear of the aircraft. He thought I was talking about the aircraft drag chute. When I clarified I was talking about my parachute, there was a moment of silence in the rear seat. He was probably thinking what kind of numbskull had he drawn as a student? He finally asked what did I want to do, abort the mission or continue on, adding that if we had to eject, I would just have an immediate opening chute! I said, "lets just continue on with the mission" which we did. What a lousy way to start a new program!

Approaching the KB-50, the IP shook the control stick saying he had the aircraft. He flew the join-up with the tanker and after receiving tanker clearance; he methodically crossed under Lead and took up the pre-contact position by the left wing basket. As he was doing all this, he provided a running commentary on what he was doing; stabilize two to three feet behind the basket with the probe lined up at the 2 o'clock position. He said as we moved forward the airflow from the nose of the F-100 would force the basket up and to the right centering it perfectly with the probe. It was obvious he had a lot of experience doing this as the probe entered and contacted the basket simultaneously as he ended his descriptive commentary. Again, picking up the commentary with the confidence of a radio ballgame announcer, he described the technique for continuing the forward momentum, pushing approximately forty feet of the fuel hose into the take-up reel in the wing pod until two small red lights on the pod turned green indicating we were transferring fuel. We were now approximately within twenty feet of the KB-50's left wing, which he explained he was using as a horizon indicator. I was amazed. I had never been this close to such a large aircraft in formation before.

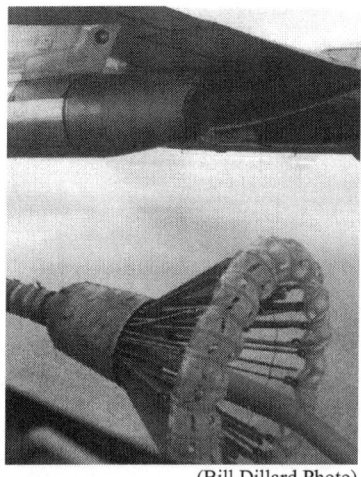

(Bill Dillard Photo)
Hooked up on Left Wing of Refueling Basket, Adding Power to Push Hose into Pod.

(Bill Dillard Photo)
Moving Forward Until Lights on KB-50 Pod Change From Red to Green Indicating Fuel Was Transferring.

The IP slowly backed away from the refueling position, disconnected, and then shook the stick saying you got the aircraft. I took control of the aircraft and I could tell I was pretty tensed up by the tight hold I had on the stick grip. For a young Lieutenant, my IP was a very good instructor. He told me to just relax and do as he did; it was easy. Don't know how he knew I was tensed up; maybe he just knew from experience and recalled his first air-to-air refueling!

Stabilized in the pre-contact position, I tried to mimic what my IP had demonstrated and to my surprise, succeeded on hooking up on my first attempt. All of a sudden, my confidence in my ability to air-refuel could not have been higher, especially after doing repeated hook-ups without any difficulty. The tension and death grip on the stick grip soon disappeared and I actually enjoyed the challenge and finesse required to get the probe into the basket. I made it a personal goal to get hooked up on the first attempt on all future air-refuelings. I never kept score, but I'd estimate that I was successful in achieving this goal around 90% of the time.

My first air refueling flight ended up the way it started. After landing, I had the dubious distinction of having to unstrap, get out of my parachute harness, climb out of the cockpit, and then standing on the ladder, gather as much of the white and orange silk of my parachute into a small enough bundle to carry it down the ladder to the ramp. It wouldn't have been so embarrassing except for the audience of crew chiefs, line chiefs and a couple of instructors from my flight standing on the ramp with expressions of bewilderment on their faces!

In the next phase of training, air-to-air gunnery, we got to shoot at an airborne target for the first time in our careers. The instructor pilot functioned as the range safety officer, tightly controlling the flight like his life depended on it and it did, as the target was only towed 1,500 feet behind his plane. In reality, if everyone abided by established procedures, the chances of hitting the tow plane were zero. But the potential was always there for a shooter to screw up; as Murphy's Law epigram states, "Anything that can go wrong will go wrong." There have been cases of the tow plane being hit! One of the principle rules was to shoot only in the turning portion of the racetrack pattern and always from the inside of the turn, firing out. This guaranteed the tow aircraft would always be in a different plane away from the target.

The target, known as a dart because of its shape, is attached to a carriage apparatus loaded on the outboard station of the tow aircraft. The tow aircraft is restricted to 250-kts with the dart in the stowed position. Upon release, the dart could be towed up to 450-kts with the cable reel pod loaded on the outboard station, or 700-kts if the pod was on the fuselage centerline.

Shooting at a target that is not only moving but also changing speed

F-100D Loaded With a Dart Target on the Outboard Station.
(Stock Photo)

was certainly much more challenging than attacking a stationary ground target. The racetrack pattern was flown with alternating diving and climbing turns. In the straightaway portion of the pattern, the dart is towed at a constant 300-Kts. The tow pilot would call 30 seconds to turn and once in the turn, he'd call "Clear to fire." The shooter had to acknowledge all tow calls and call coming off the target. Ten seconds before the tow started his turn, the shooter would start his roll-in from an off-set perch 3,000 feet above and 3,000 to 5,000 feet behind the dart and if done properly, almost be at firing parameters when the clear to fire call would be received.

The F-100's A-4 gun-sight provided automatic target radar lock-on with range and lead computations. All we had to do in order to successfully score a hit was smoothly put and keep the pipper tracking on the dart a couple of seconds when we got within range of 6,000 feet down to 600 feet, a task much easier said than done for an inexperienced student. The first few times I did the attacking maneuver, it all seemed so quick like I was in and off in just a few seconds. After a few flights, especially after I got a few hits, it was like the light came on! I became more aware of my surroundings and got rid of that time compression sensation of my earlier flights. In order to qualify in the dart, we had to score a hit 50 percent of the time.

This became a problem for me and my good friend George Gifford in the early Dart phase. We both needed one more hit in our running string of hits and misses to qualify. In the next mission, we each thought we had gotten a hit but unfortunately, the tow pilot was unable to release and drop the dart in the recovery area along the side of the outside runway at Nellis. He ended up having to drag the dart off on a small knoll northwest of the field. At the debrief, we both claimed a hit but the instructor would not accept it because it wasn't verifiable (a good dart pilot can usually feel the dart getting hit). Guess he must have felt sorry for George and me or he just wanted to send us on a wild goose chase because he told us if we were willing to go out to the knoll, find the dart and verify for sure that we had hit it, he would give us credit in our grade books as dart qualified. Each dart was spray painted with an identification number, which he gave us and said it should be easy to find the dart because he could tell us exactly where he had dragged it off on the knoll. George and I looked at each other and agreed to go look for it that weekend.

That Saturday turned out to be a real fiasco when George and I drove out to the knoll in the desert in search of our dart. It was a good thing it was winter because the knoll was much further than it looked from where we had to park the car and start hiking. When we reached the base of the knoll, we were also surprised by the number of darts lying around all over the place. We started climbing to where we were told we would find our dart, checking each dart we passed just in case the instructor was mistaken on its exact location. After working up hours of sweat searching all over the knoll, we both agreed it was time to give up and accept the fact now it was going to take two more sorties with hits to qualify.

That Monday, we reported we were unable to locate our dart to verify we had hit it. To our surprise and relief, our IP informed us we still only needed one more hit since the last mission was considered a "non-counter" because the dart wasn't recovered. We both did qualify in the dart but I don't recall if either George or I got a hit on the next mission or if it was later missions in which we qualified.

The final training phase introduced us to low-level navigation and realistic ground attack tactics on an uncontrolled tactical gunnery range. One of my first exposures to low-level tactical flying was led by Capt.

William "Higgy" Higginbotham. "Higgy" was a highly experienced instructor who liked to push the envelope. On this specific mission, I flew his wing as number two as he led us on a low level recce mission, weaving the flight back and forth across a rural road at 300 feet and 360-kts out in the desert northwest of Las Vegas. I was impressed and thought this was what being a fighter pilot was all about! The road led us to the tactical range where we followed "Higgy" as he climbed over the range and rolled in for a dive-bombing attack on a mock airfield with parked derelict airframes in dirt revetments. We did multiple attacks until we were rid of all our bombs. This was such a change from the boxed patterns flown at controlled ranges; much more realistic training.

Higginbotham was very vocal about wanting to be a "Thunderbird." He tried out for the team after we graduated and became a "Thunderbird," flying with the team during the 1963 and 1964 season.

(Stock Photo)

A Thunderbird F-100D, Most Recognizable F-100 Paint Scheme.

I now look back at this time in my career and realize how lucky I was to survive my early aviation years. I was young, naïve, with limited experience flying on the feathered edge. Finally, at Nellis I experienced a wake up call and realized there was a potential for early personal mortality in this career. I was scheduled for a solo single ship low-level navigation flight ending with a nuclear weapon delivery at the range. After detailed preparation and ready to step to the airplane, we were placed on a temporary hold due to weather. A couple of us sat around the pilot's ready room discussing the long road we had traveled to become fighter pilots. We were almost at the end of all the training, would be graduating shortly and reporting to our first operational squadrons. We certainly were pleased with ourselves and confident we could handle a little weather. Finally, the weather hold was lifted and we stepped to our planes. Although we were solo, we were all flying on the same mission frequency. Flying in valleys at 300 feet and 360-kts, would put us way below the towering mountain ridges on each side of our route. Some of these valleys were boxed canyons requiring us to climb and pop over the ridge on to the next valley. It was an enjoyable adrenaline rush. The cloud cover, which initially was a couple thousand feet above the mountaintops, started getting lower as the route progressed. I figured if it got too bad, I would just do a 180 and abort the mission. Unfortunately, by the time I made the decision to abort, I was in a boxed canyon too narrow in which to turn and I was staring at a mountain ridge buried half way in the clouds in front of me. I momentarily panicked, not knowing what to do. I finally took the only option available, selected afterburner and pulled to a 30-degree climb hoping I'd clear the mountains in front of me. The entire time I was in the clouds I was deathly afraid I was going to hit the ridge.

Once on top of the clouds, I realized how close I had come to becoming a statistic. This is how accidents happen! I survived not because of skill and cunning, but rather because of luck or Saint Thérèse of Lisieux, the patron saint of pilots was looking over me.

Chapter 2: Survival Training

The Stead AFB Survival Training School was established in mid-1951 during the Korean War. Twenty-one American service men refused repatriation at the end of the war in 1953. They had been successfully indoctrinated or "brainwashed" into believing that Communism was a better way of life and they chose a new life in Communist China over returning home to their families in the United States. One common thread among these men was they were all lower rank enlisted with a low education. But more disturbing was the number of officers with higher levels of education who conducted themselves less than honorably while in captivity.

By 1961, when I reported to Stead AFB, Reno, Nevada, in early December, the curriculum had incorporated lessons learned from POW experiences and behavior in the Korean War. The curriculum's major objectives of training aircrew on how to survive in the wilderness until rescued, and evasion/escape techniques in hostile territory were expanded to include instruction in the proper conduct as a Prisoner of War (POW) in case of capture.

The first two weeks of the three-week course were all academics and led to the field exercise the final week. We were taught The Code of Conduct's six articles through class discussion. It was not just a case of memorizing each article; we had to understand the rationale for its existence. Utilizing case studies from the Korean Conflict, the instructors provided real world examples that necessitated the adoption of these articles in the Code of Conduct.

Tied to the Code of Conduct, we were taught the rights of prisoners protected by the Geneva Convention. This was a difficult subject for the instructor to teach with conviction; practically every article of the Geneva Convention was met with student skepticism that these rules would likely NOT be recognized or adhered to by most of our potential enemies. Ironically just four years later, our experiences in Vietnam proved us right!

We also received training on techniques for responding to interrogation. It is very easy to get tripped up on reexamination when trying to lie to an interrogator. Putting a little bit of truth in your response makes it easier to recall what you've said previously and helps give a consistent reply when asked the same or similar question again under duress.

By the end of our first week, we all knew what to expect if we were ever captured. Unfortunately, I don't believe it was anything like what our POWs in Vietnam expected.

The second week of academics covered how to survive in the hinterlands. For the outdoor types, I'm sure there was only a limited amount of new information to absorb, but for a city slicker like me who'd never been camping, the instruction was very informative. By the end of the week, I was confident I could survive in a remote unfriendly environment, at least for a little while. Five years later, I was able to put some of this training to actual use.

At conclusion of the final class, we were issued survival gear we had to pack over the weekend in preparation for being bussed to the exercise area in the Sierra Nevada Mountains. The area received a record snowfall over the weekend making it the coldest winter with the deepest snowdrifts in 14 years!

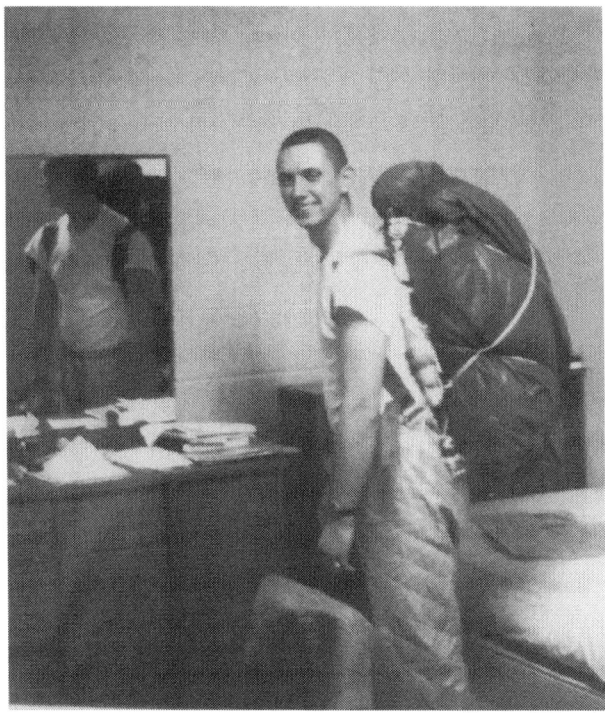

Author, Packed and Ready For Survival Training in the Wilderness, Stead AFB, Reno, Nevada

(Personal Photo)

It was miserably cold when we arrived at the drop off point. Low clouds blocked any sunrays and the ground was covered with patches of fog and everyone's exhaling breath visible in the cold air. We all had our arms crossed in front of our chest stomping our feet trying to stay warm as we were split into small groups of six to eight students for assignment to NCO field instructors. Each group took off to claim a patch of woods to set up camp for the night. Our NCO guided us while we made a shelter and mattress using a parachute, tree branches, and pine needles. We had to introduce ourselves and provide a little background about who we were. It was obvious my instructor picked me out as the city slicker and he assigned me the task of killing our dinner for the night, a small rabbit he pulled out of a cage. He held the rabbit by the ears and pointed where on the neck I needed to apply a stiff karate chop for an instant kill. I failed to achieve that instant kill when I hit the rabbit's neck and was left holding a rabbit with a spastically jerking body. The NCO was not only unimpressed, he was extremely unhappy. He took the jerking rabbit and put it out of its misery with one sharp karate chop. After that he kept picking on me for different tasks that further emphasized my lack of outdoor experience. I definitely got the impression he did not like me and his less than glowing final remarks on my training form confirmed my suspicion.

The next morning, we woke up to a beautiful clear day. We had a minimal breakfast consisting of strips of beef jerky, an apple or orange, and coffee. I picked an orange for breakfast, as I was a non-meat eater nor coffee drinker. Not having eaten any rabbit the evening before and with not much of a breakfast, I was starting to feel really hungry by the time we got paired up for a long distance survival and evasion trek through the woods of the Sierra Nevada.

We were briefed on what we could and could not do during our one-way excursion, given a rudimentary map with a route to a safe area, a small compass, and a card, which we had to present on demand if we were caught before reaching the safe area. The opposition forces would punch the card to record how many times you'd been caught trying to reach safety. The trek to the safe area was distant enough through wild country that we were given 36 hours to reach it.

As luck would have it, my partner was a young gong-ho 1st Lt. who had just completed jump school before reporting to Survival School. Of course this put him in much better physical shape than me. He volunteered to break trail and lead for three hours through the heavy snow, and then we'd switch positions. The snow was sufficiently deep and powdery that we really should have been equipped with snowshoes, but what pilot would be flying a fighter and have snowshoes as part of their survival equipment? So we broke trail in flight boots and sank up to just below the knees; it was a very arduous task.

At mid-day, we were launched on our adventure. My Lt. started out like a scalded ape, breaking trail as if we were in a race to beat everyone else to the safe area. I figured he would settle down to a more manageable pace after awhile but after the first hour, I had to suggest we slow down a bit to conserve our energy. Saying he felt fine, he asked how I was doing? Since he was doing the hardest part of breaking trail, I didn't want to come across as a wuss, and answered I was okay, so we kept going at a killer pace that in my opinion was far too fast.

I figured the only way I was going to survive was to hang tough until it was my turn to break trail and then set my own pace. Finally, when I said it was my turn to lead, the Lt. declined saying he was still feeling fresh! I could not convince him to let me take the lead and I was too tired to argue, so he broke trail for almost six hours! I could tell he was finally getting tired the last hour as his pace had slowed quite a bit. He finally fell forward onto the snow exhausted as he tried to lift his leg out of the snow on his last step.

By now it was starting to get dark and colder as the sun disappeared behind the mountains. I was so relieved we had to stop while he picked himself off the snow, it gave me a chance to take a short rest before I started breaking trail. After a couple of minutes of catching our breaths, I stepped around him to take up the lead, took about three steps breaking trail, and fell flat on my face dead tired. He had drained us both out of energy, we were beat, thirsty, and in the center of a clearing in the open without a tree or brush for concealment! We had used all our water keeping ourselves hydrated during our six-hour exhaustive pace. We dug a small hole in the snow until we hit dirt, scraped together a few dead pine needles that were on the ground, and lit them with the Lt.'s lighter; this was one of the don'ts on which we had been briefed. The school was very concerned over the potential of starting any forest fires. We held our snow filled canteens over the small flame in the hole to melt into drinking water. After we melted the snow, we made sure we put out the fire and quickly covered the hole with snow, mindful of the briefing about not using any fire while on the trek.

The water not only quenched our thirst but the time it took for us to get it also rejuvenated the energy to march on. The Lt. insisted on leading again saying we were very close to where we had planned to spend the night, which was about the mid-way point to our destination.

Although it was a beautiful clear moonlit night, in the thick woods it was fairly dark. By now, it was rather late and we figured we should be getting close to our planned stop for the night. Suddenly, we came upon an unexpected major paved road! We stood at the edge of the woods and the road trying to read our map in the moonlight when we heard a match on the other side of the road being struck. Staring in the direction of the noise, we saw the lit match move and illuminate a parka covered face as the match neared the cigarette in its lips, heavily shielded from the cold and a rifle slung across the back. We just stood there frozen, not knowing what to do! After a moment, the soldier waved us across the road and motioned the direction in which we should continue without saying a word. We happily followed his direction, figuring the soldier probably felt it was too cold and not worth the effort to take off his glove, reach in his pocket and get his hole punch to record we had been caught. I thought what miserable duty that must have been to stand guard all night long in the cold just to punch someone's card and then let them go!

Across the road we were back in the dark woods again with a less strenuous hike in shallower snow. Reaching the edge of the next clearing, we decided this was a good place to bed down for the night. I discovered a large fallen tree lying half covered in snow with an open crevice underneath it large enough for me to crawl into. I told my teammate I was going to use it as my shelter as he was searching for his spot to sleep. I was so tired I fell asleep as soon as I curled up in the fetal position without knowing where the Lt. ended up.

I must have really been worn out as I slept solidly through the entire night and only awoke when I heard the loud sound of helicopter blades beating up the air. Through half opened slits for eyes, I spotted a low flying H-19 helicopter traversing the clearing we were near. When it was all clear, I crawled out from beneath the tree shelter and after a short time, I met back up with my partner. The sound of the helicopter had also awakened him. We studied our map and got reoriented again using the small compass preparing to pick up the trek again. It was a bright clear day and our next checkpoint was across the clearing. We dared not take the chance of being seen walking across the clearing. We agreed to go deeper into the woods and make it more difficult of being spotted as we followed the perimeter to get to the other side.

We successfully reached our checkpoint where we were briefed we'd be met by partisans with food and water. In the last 20 or so hours, we had not seen any of our other classmates during our hike getting to this location; I was surprised by the number of teams coming out of the woods, many arriving around the same time. The instructors acting as partisans handed out apples and oranges and refilled our water canteens as their leader briefed the next leg. We were told we needed to separate and travel individually because the number of enemy search parties had drastically increased and our chances of reaching the safe area were better traveling alone. Our maps were confiscated on the pretext that they should not fall into enemy hands. In reality, from this point forward, the route became more of an obstacle course, clearly marked and funneling us not into a safe zone but capture and the POW camp.

After a short rest period, we were sent off again. Nothing out of the ordinary happened in the early portion of the course, just lots of climbing over or zigzagging around various obstacles, and ducking and hiding from GI's patrolling sections of the course. The further into the course, the more difficult and challenging it became to avoid getting caught. While hiding, I could hear people being captured. I was within visual sight of the POW camp, its bright security lights glowing in the distance. It was now dark and I was agonizingly hungry, cold, and tired. Getting caught could have possibly ended this but I wasn't sure. Also, the fact that I had a clean capture card with no holes punched, was a motivator to try and reach the POW camp with a clean card.

I continued on, sometimes crawling in the dark as I got closer to areas occasionally lit up by sweeping search lights. I finally reached the last obstacle, a very deep ravine with sides that were almost vertical. On the other side of the ravine, it was only a short walk to enter the guarded gate of the POW camp.

I crawled to the edge of the ravine and looked inside checking to the right and left for any threats. It was awfully dark and hard to see in the shadows but I thought it was clear. I started a slow half climb, half slide down the near vertical wall, suddenly, I heard and saw a match get lit directly below me! I struggled to stop my movement downward as I spotted a soldier directly beneath my feet, his head slightly bent down lighting his cigarette. Grabbing any small crevice or indent I could use as hand and foot holds in the wall I was able to stop, but I knew there was no way he could miss hearing and feeling the dirt and small pebbles that continued to rain down after I had stopped. He just stayed leaning against the ravine wall directly below me smoking his cigarette. After awhile, he flicked the cigarette to the ground, picked up his rifle he had leaned next to him, and snuffed the cigarette out with his foot as he flung the rifle and walked off. I seriously felt he knew I was there and was just enjoying making me strain to keep from sliding down on top of him.

I slid to the ravine floor, ran across to the opposite wall, climbed out and walked into the POW camp. Immediately I was lined up with a bunch of other POW classmates and forced to stand at attention shivering in the freezing cold waiting to be interrogated. One by one, the first man in line would disappear into the building in front of us. Finally, it was my turn as I was escorted into a room that was nice and warm. The guard sat me down in front of a large desk and left leaving me alone with a clean cut man in a uniform with a red star on each lapel on the other side of the desk. He asked for my name, rank, and serial number and I provided only this information in accordance with the Code of Conduct. He followed up in a very friendly way asking where I was from. I remained silent. What did my parents do was the next question. Again I just sat there. He lit a cigarette and offered it to me and I refused saying I didn't smoke. He continued on making friendly small talk trying to get me to respond. When I wouldn't speak with him, he informed me he wanted me to be treated fairly but that I was making it very hard for myself. He got up and left me sitting there alone. It was obvious he was trying to make me nervous which was difficult to do knowing I was not captured and I was just in a training situation. After a little while, another guy in a similar uniform entered from behind my chair and slapped me behind the head as he passed me going to his chair. I started thinking, "Oh oh, here comes the bad cop!" He sat down and immediately ordered me to strip down to my shorts. After stripping down, the room wasn't so nice and warm anymore. He conducted his entire interrogation with me wearing only my shorts. I couldn't help but smile as I pictured him sitting on the john with his shorts wrapped around his ankles, a technique taught in class for trying to put yourself on an equal basis with the interrogator. He asked me what I thought was so funny? I replied, "Oh nothing". That ended the questioning, he grabbed me by the arm and led me to a door on the opposite side of where I had entered, and threw me out onto the snow, still only in my shorts! My clothes soon followed and I had to get dress outside in the cold, being watched by a guard who led me away to my assigned barracks, if you wanted to call it that.

The building was a square shaped single bay with a bunch of bunk beds each topped with a wool cover. The building wasn't heated other than the body heat of the mass of humanity squeezed into the tight quarters, so we slept in our clothes, which were getting pretty ripe by now. After lights out, the bay remained pretty well illuminated because of the bright security floodlights that shone through the windows. At lights out, loud Asian music began blaring throughout the camp and lasted most of the night making it difficult to fall asleep. During the day, the Asian music was replaced with a shrilling Asian voice propagandizing the virtues of Communism.

The following morning, we were mustered out in front of the building into a formation for roll call. I was in the front line of POWs marched off to another building, leaving the rest of the formation standing at attention in the freezing cold. In the other building, we were forced into and locked in small black boxes. The only way one could fit into the restricted space was to sit with legs crammed against one's chest and head bent down. It was extremely uncomfortable with an inability to shift weight or body position, especially if you were a large person. Luckily, I was small and slim and had no problem fitting in the dark box. Anyone with a tinge of claustrophobia was in trouble! After 30 to 40 minutes, the door opened and two guards pulled me out. When I stood right up, they pushed me back in the box, saying I needed more time. Fortunately, as I was being pushed back into my box, I saw the prisoner in the next box fall to the ground with wobbly legs. I quickly surmised his legs probably had fallen asleep and had no feelings because of the cramped position in the small space. After another ten minutes in the box, I heard the guards' voices on the other side of the door as they started opening it. This time I was prepared to show them what they anticipated seeing. When my feet hit the ground, I intentionally let my legs continue towards the ground falling to my knees. When the guards tried to lift me back onto my feet, I continued on with my act as if my legs were asleep, truly an Oscar winning performance!

This physical harassment was the closest example of "torture" we experienced. After each POW had their turn in the box, we were marched back to our barracks area and were left alone to just pace around our building trying to keep warm. After the black box exercise, with the exception of the shrill voice over the loud speakers rivaling the sound of fingernails screeching across a black board, it got kind of boring with nothing much to do.

Occasionally, in an attempt to gross us out, we were fed bizarre food such as grasshoppers or raw octopus. It would have been more effective if they hadn't used delicacy flavored samples out of jars purchased in markets.

The POW exercise lasted two and a half days. The greatest challenge was battling the extreme cold temperature. As important as it was to experience what it would be like to be a captive, there is no way to achieve the realism of physical torture and the devastating uncertainty associated with not knowing how long one will be held captive or if one will ever be repatriated.

The curriculum reflected the last war fought and training emphasis was on the individual fighting man. In Vietnam, our captives' resistance was a group effort directed by a disciplined command structure, the 4th Allied Prisoner of War Wing, formed by Lieutenant General John P. Flynn, the senior ranking POW, something that was not taught in the 1961 course.

Chapter 3: Reporting to the Donald Duck Squadron

With a couple of cross-country sorties left before graduating from the F-100 Advanced Gunnery Course, we had already received our follow-on first operational assignments. It was astonishing, the base assignments were such that each student got their choice of base. Jerry Stamps and I had been together since Primary Flight Training and had become good friends; we chose the two assignments to George AFB, in Victorville, California. George had two fighter wings, the 31st and the 479th Tactical Fighter Wings. Our orders were to the 31st, the F-100 wing but we had visions of working our way into the 479th equipped with the F-104.

Returning from one of my last flights, I was surprised to see my wife on the other side of the chain-link fence separating the flight line and the rest of the base. After shutting down, I climbed out of the cockpit and walked over hoping there wasn't anything wrong. As I reached her, she informed me our orders had been changed. The 31st Wing was being transferred to Homestead AFB, Florida and we were to report there instead! We were disappointed since George was only a little over two hours from home and family; now we were going to be over 2,700 miles on the opposite coast.

Upon completion of my Nellis F-100 Advanced Gunnery training, we packed up our 1960 Pontiac Ventura, the wife riding shotgun and the two kids in back on a crib mattress covering a piece of plywood sized to fit between the front bench seat and the rear seat. The boys were good little travelers and kept each other entertained in this playpen-like area as we traveled cross-country from Las Vegas, Nevada, to Homestead AFB at the southern tip of Florida. This was in the days before most American car manufacture's offered seat belts and before the Interstates were completed. It was our third trip across the states and 400 miles longer than our first trip from Los Angeles to Moultrie, Georgia, only two years earlier when this whole process to eventually become a fighter pilot started. I'd been in the Air Force 25 months and had already put the family through six moves! I was finally headed for what I had been trained to do...be an operational F-100 pilot.

There was an advantage to reporting directly to Homestead. As part of the in processing, I checked with housing and asked for off-base housing referrals. The clerked behind the counter asked, "Don't you want to live on base?" I asked, "There's base housing available?" He replied in the affirmative. I was totally shocked, never thinking I would qualify for base housing as a 1st Lieutenant. We ended up being able to choose between two houses and were settled in by the time the Wing showed up several weeks later. When the entire Wing had arrived, there were Majors who had to live off base because by then base housing had been filled up.

Homestead AFB was a Strategic Air Command (SAC) base with B-52 bombers; the 31st TFW and its four fighter squadrons were going to be tenants on the base. Jerry and I were assigned to the 309th Tactical Fighter Squadron with lineage going back to World War II when the squadron was known as the "Wild Ducks". In the mid-fifties, the squadron emblem was modernized with Walt Disney's "Donald Duck".

(Personal Photo)
309th Tac Ftr Sqdn Patch circa mid 1950's

The complete transfer from George to Homestead took two months so by the time I got my first flight with the squadron, it had been 69 days since my last F-100 flight. But I was with the big boys now and I was put up for my first tactical Standard Evaluation (Stan Eval) check ride only six flights after my initial flight in the 309th.

46

(Personal Photo)
309th Huns on Homestead AFB, FL, Runway Ready for Take-OFF

    I briefed the High-Low-High mission to Avon Park Gunnery Range in the center of Florida for a nuclear delivery using a 25-pound Mk-76 training bomb. The Stan Eval check pilot and I walked out to our "F" in plenty of time so I wouldn't feel rushed. I did my pre-flight of the aircraft with plenty of time to spare. Capt. Snowden, the check pilot, said he was going to step away fifty feet from the plane and have a smoke since we still had time before engine start. I joined him and we sat on the ramp while he had his smoke. I was staring at the jet thinking about the mission when all of a sudden I realized I had not set the LABS bombing gyro under the saddleback panel behind the cockpit! I jumped and ran over to the jet, climbed up on the wing, and leaning against the fuselage, I set the gyro just in time before having to climb into the front cockpit. After that little embarrassing episode, I flew the mission as briefed and got a qualifying LABS bomb hit.

    At the flight debrief, Snowden told me how glad he was I remembered to set the gyro, even if it was at the last minute, otherwise he might have had to bust me on the ride. After debriefing the good and bad points of

(Stock Photo)

Hun With Saddle Back Panel Removed and Propped on Aircraft Spine Providing Access to LABS Gyro Setting by Pilot.

the mission, Snowden signed my Stan Eval form as qualified. I had just passed my first tactical Stan Eval of my career.

Snowden was a good guy. He called me later that afternoon to let me know that in all his check rides he'd ever given, I was the first pilot he had ever seen come close to forgetting to set the gyro. But the reason he was calling was he was amused and couldn't get over the fact that his afternoon check ride did forget and delivered his bomb using my setting from the previous flight! I kiddingly asked him about his bomb hit, was it qualifying?

In the Advanced Gunnery Training program at Nellis, the centerline station was always clean (empty), the practice munitions loaded on a rack attached to the outboard pylon. At Homestead, we flew with a SUU-21 bomb dispenser loaded on the centerline station. This configuration disabled the speed brake, as the cut out in the center of the speed brake was not large enough to clear the bomb dispenser in the extended position. Not having an operable speed brake was definitely a handicap for an F-100 pilot with limited experience and required a more cautious approach to precise speed management. Under preplanned situations, one could slow down to landing gear lowering speed and use the landing gear as a drag device in the TACAN holding pattern and penetration. However, this technique was not useable when an unpredicted requirement for rapid speed reduction arose.

Pair of 309th TFS Clean Hun's With Speed Brakes Extended.
(309th TFS Photo)

**Landing Gear Used as Drag Device in Lieu of
Speed Brakes for TACAN Penetration.**
(Personal Photo)

In due time, an imaginative enlisted maintenance individual submitted through the Air Force Suggestion Program, an idea to enlarge the speed brake notch sufficiently to clear the SUU bomb dispenser when the speed brake was extended. The suggestion was approved and the speed brake was modified throughout the F-100 fleet.

In 1962, Tactical Air Command (TAC) was not nearly as regimented as SAC. In contrast to SAC personnel who conducted themselves in an utmost serious and professional manner, TAC individuals, especially fighter pilots, performed their duties with a freewheeling flamboyant spirit. The old heads in the squadron were friendly but they sure weren't going to give away their trade secrets they'd learned through years of experience. Flight debriefings were short and not very helpful in accelerating the new guy's learning curve. In close formation, the wingman aligns Lead's wing tip light on the center of the fuselage star insignia. In briefings, the cynical instruction, half jokingly, half seriously, given new wingmen was "Keep the light on the star and shut up." This reflected the attitude among a lot of the guys who had been in the squadron a long time.

At Homestead, with less than 200 F-100 hours, I was competing against pilots with a couple of thousand hours of F-100 experience. The largest disparity was most evident in the air-to-air arena. In operational Aircraft Combat Maneuvering (ACM) training missions, the squadron old heads were constantly at the six o'clock position simulating gunning the new guys' brains out. In debriefings, I'd ask how did you get at my six so fast? What am I doing wrong? No matter what old head I had flown with, the stock answer was always the same; "Don't worry, with a little experience, you'll get the hang of it!"

One day after engine start, my Lead radioed he was aborting and instructed me to go out to the MOA and get some flying time. Immediately after taking-off, I received a call on Guard Channel to come up Squadron Common frequency. I checked in on the squadron frequency and it was Don Castleman, one of the squadron old heads. He informed me that his wingman had just aborted and told me to join up over the field and we'd go bump heads (dogfight). Such was the fluidity of TAC in those days that two individuals could join up and fly an extremely dynamic mission without even having briefed with each other!

Once in the MOA, we set up for our first engagement around 20,000 feet, each taking a 45-degree split away to separate. After flying to where we were almost out of sight of each other, Don called for us to reverse. Approaching at a closing rate of 800-kts, he called "fights on" as we passed each other. The sign of an inexperienced fighter pilot is a tendency to fight in the horizontal plane. I was beyond that and had learned to go into the vertical; I pulled up as we crossed. After several vertical turns, Don had done his magic and was in his usual position at my six o'clock. At least it had taken him a few more turns than usual to get into gun firing position.

We set up for a second engagement. After a few vertical turns, Don had again worked his way into my rear cone, but he had not yet reached the six o'clock position. I could see him at my 7:30 as I was still climbing in the near vertical in an ever so slight left bank. For the first time in an ACM engagement with someone of his experience, I felt if I could just pull a little harder towards Don, I could spit him to the outside of our turning fight. I pulled a little harder and got the last little bit of "G" available with 200-kts. Unfortunately, I must have subconsciously applied a little bit of left aileron causing the plane to yaw right because of the F-100's adverse yaw phenomenon. The aircraft started to roll right at a rapidly increasing rate. At Luke, they taught us to avoid this regime of flight and that if we experienced adverse yaw, we should let go of the control stick as soon as possible; if done early enough, the aircraft would recover itself and avoid entering an uncontrollable maneuver.

I immediately let go of the stick but it must not have been quick enough. The aircraft tumbled tail over nose violently several times, scaring the hell out of me. When the aircraft recovered by itself, Don was at my dead 12 o'clock. I quickly grabbed the control stick and started flying the airplane again. I keyed the mic button and called out over the radio, "Rat-tat-tat-tat," mimicking a machine gun, finishing up with, "Smile, you're on camera!"

Don rocked his wings and finished with a right wing dip signaling me to join up on his right wing. When I got on his wing, he looked over at me shaking his head as if wondering how the hell did I do that and end up at his six.

On the ramp, Don hurried over to walk back to our Ops building together. The first thing he asked was, "Okay, what did you do and how did you do it?" It gave me great pleasure to say, "Don't worry, you'll pick it up with more experience". Don just smiled and after that flight, we became closer friends.

Three years later, I came across Don sitting at the Yokota Officer's Club bar having a drink. It had been about two years since I'd last seen

Don when I left Homestead to check out in the F-105. Don was stationed at some remote site in Japan and was TDY to Yokota for a few days to get his annual physical. I arranged to take him up in an F-105F during his few days at Yokota. While giving him a dollar tour of the local area, he brought up that flight where I had tumbled the F-100 and spit him out in front of me. I was surprised he still remembered that flight, it must have made an impression because he again asked what happened that day, what had I done. I told him, "Don, you're not going to believe this, but I got into adverse yaw, let go of the stick and scared the hell out of myself when that thing tumbled…and was surprised to find you right in front of me when she recovered." He banged his fist against the canopy saying, "I knew it, I just couldn't believe my eyes when I went zipping by you with that 100 looking like it had momentarily stopped in mid-air. I had never seen anything like that before".

(Stock Photo)
Okinawa Island, 1962 309th TFS Deployment to Kadena AB.

In mid-July, only six weeks after my first F-100 flight at Homestead, the 309th deployed for a three-month rotation to Kadena AB, Okinawa. While I was in pilot training, an instructor had asked me what I hoped to get as an assignment upon graduating. When I said I wanted fighters in Tactical Air Command, he raised his eyebrows and said, "You're going to be gone an awful lot". At the time, it didn't sound so bad and I thought flying fighters would be worth it. Now having to say goodbye to my twenty-three year old wife and two sons only 30 and 15 months old, wasn't as easy as I thought. This was the first of several lengthy separations in our career. I say "our" because it was a joint family effort.

Several of us were flown over on a "crowd killer" while the old heads ferried the Huns to Kadena. We were there to hold down the nuclear alert commitment of the 18th TFW whose pilots were at Nellis AFB TDY checking out in the new F-105.

It was fairly late and dark when we arrived at Kadena with hardly anything visible except for security floodlights on the ramp and some lit buildings throughout the base. There was a very unfamiliar scent in the air mixed with the ocean smell of being on an island. I was anxious for daylight so I could see what Okinawa really looked like.

The following day was beautifully clear with a deep blue sky closely matching the nearby ocean. We were assigned a building for our Squadron Operations on the flight line close to Base Operations and near aircraft parking spots located on three different tiers. Our first task was to become qualified Bomb Commanders certified on the nuclear targets assigned to the 18th TFW and relieve the last remaining Kadena pilots sitting nuclear alert. The certification process consisted of passing a "murder board" after studying mission folders of targets individually assigned to a specific pilot. We were required to brief from memory, the specific details of the mission heading, time, minimum IFR altitude, and fuel remaining for each navigation leg to the target; demonstrate complete knowledge of the aircraft's and special weapon's switchology, and show the board we could fly the mission and reach the target without the mission folder.

We quickly assumed responsibility for the nuclear alert commitment. The nuclear loaded F-100's on the alert pad were all 18th TFW birds. The Kadena pilot I was relieving and I went out to his aircraft to change out our personal equipment. He had me get in the cockpit and quickly went over all the switches and how they should all be set up for launching from a nuclear alert posture. As he talked me through all the switches, I was surprised when we got to the right side console as it was configured with a Doppler Navigation system with which I was totally unfamiliar. When he briefed me on how to use the system, it was so quick and so much information, it was like being fed through a huge fire hose. I was overwhelmed! Being a Bomb Commander on nuclear alert is an awesome responsibility. My unfamiliarity with the Doppler system and uncertainty on how to employ it knocked my confidence with which I passed the murder board down a notch or two. But I still believed I could successfully fly the mission if need be, after all, I had proven to the murder board that I knew how to get to the target using just time and distance.

At Kadena, I flew with 450-gallon wing tanks for the first time. These were the original long-range external fuel tanks, known as "tubs", quite large with a high drag coefficient. Because of their high drag, more streamlined 275-gallon tanks were designed for everyday use. These were later expanded to a 335-gallon capacity with the addition of a three

(Stock Photo)

F-100D With 450-Gallon Wing Tanks.

foot section and were the type of wing tanks we used at Homestead.

On my first flight at Kadena, the flight Lead covered the procedures for flying with the 450-gallon tanks. His briefing emphasized the need for the special weapons release handle to be extended out in order to be able to jettison the 450's. At least, that is what I thought I heard briefed. This requirement/procedure struck me as strange but since this was my first experience flying with this configuration, I did not question what I thought I had heard. When I got out to my airplane, I checked the

54

special weapons release handle and it wasn't safety wired in like they were at Homestead. If it had been safety wired, it would have made what I thought I had heard briefed even more suspicious.

I flew the orientation mission as briefed, learning the local area, and getting the feel of the 450-tank configuration.

Three days later, I had my second flight, this time in an "F" with the squadron maintenance officer in the rear seat. He was a rated pilot but he was never on the flying schedule in a "D" so I never knew if he was current in the F-100. We were configured with a centerline SUU-21 practice bomb dispenser with six practice bombs and two 450-gallon wing tanks. For the second time in three days, I pulled the special weapons handle out as I took the runway for take-off. The gunnery range was a little less than 30 miles northeast of Kadena. I set up the weapons switches for a simulated nuclear lay down release and approached the target at 200 feet and Mach 0.70. When I pickled (pressed the bomb release button), I felt a thump like something much larger than a five-pound Mk-106 high drag practice bomb left the airplane!

I left all the switches the way they were set and returned to Kadena and landed with a missing SUU-21. I was asked why the special weapons handle was extended. I learned my explanation of having to have it out when configured with 450-gallon tanks in case they needed to be jettisoned was erroneous. I felt like a real dummy but was surprised at the squadron's reaction. It was like it was no big deal, just another learning experience for the new guy.

I thought the incident had passed but about a week later, an acquaintance from my ROTC university days spotted me having dinner at the Officer's Club and asked if he could join me. We had not seen each other since graduating from school a little over two years ago. After completing all the niceties of protocol getting reacquainted, he informed me he knew I was on Okinawa and was wondering if we would cross paths. He let me know he had signed off the loss of the SUU-21 in the "Broken Arrow" report that had to be sent to higher headquarters! Broken Arrow being the Air Force's code name for a nuclear accident, I asked him how the loss of the SUU-21 qualified as a "Broken Arrow". He said since I was performing a practice nuclear weapon delivery, and the intended practice bomb was simulating a retarded nuclear weapon, the base had treated and reported the incident as a "Broken Arrow". I just nodded my head in astonishment; talk about an overreaction! Decades later, I researched lists of "Broken Arrow" reports and could not find the Kadena report among the 32 reported accidents on the supposedly complete list of "Broken Arrows".

I was flying quite regularly during my first deployment, getting 14 flights with 24 hours in the first full month. My fifteenth flight was a 5 hour and 10 minute day/night mission where we mid-air refueled off a KB-50 at night. Lead took the left wing refueling position while I took the right on the KB-50. With the F-100 refueling probe being on the right wing, this put me inside of the KB-50 wing tip close to its fuselage. It was a clear night with a partial moon. Stabilized in the pre-contact position, I was cleared in by the tanker to hook up with the drogue. I applied a little bit of power to slowly move in and got the probe into the basket on my first attempt. I pushed the refueling hose into the wing pod until the two small red lights on the pod changed from red to green indicating I was taking on fuel. I was so pleased I made it look so easy. Stabilized taking on fuel, I was focused on the tanker's wing, using it as the artificial horizon to maintain wings level. I could feel myself starting to tense up, squeezing the stick grip harder and harder. Staring at the wing, I notice a slight oscillation developing which moved the Hun above and then below the KB's wing slightly. I subconsciously and instinctively tried to cancel the slight oscillation with my pitch control, but this only made it worse as I quickly got out of sequence with it. My plane started pitching up and then down in ever increasing oscillations as I got into what pilots call a "JC" maneuver...."JESUS CHRIST!"

I immediately retarded the throttle as I tried to back away from the refueling position and disconnect from the basket before I tore it or my probe off. Meanwhile the KB-50 scanner in the side bubble window is screaming "emergency break away, emergency break away"! I succeeded in disconnecting without tearing anything off either plane.

Stabilized in the pre-contact position again, the scanner waited for the flailing refueling hose to settle down and then cleared me to the contact position. If I felt tensed up before, I was tense two or three fold now! I repeated the hook up slightly more abruptly and less smoothly than my first contact. I tried to relax and slow my actions, especially my movements with the control stick. I could feel my heart beating faster and harder as I pushed the refueling hose into the refueling position. With the green lights indicating I was taking on fuel again, I tried to not fixate on the KB-50 wing and looked at an overall larger picture of the entire wing. Although it seemed like an eternity to me trying to complete the fuel off load, the ever so small oscillations started again within a few minutes of being hooked up. I did another "emergency break away" but this time the sine wave I was going through as I backed away from the tanker was even larger and scarier than the first time. I saw much more of the top and bottom of the KB-50 this time; it was a miracle I didn't have 20 or more feet of refueling hose still attached to the probe by the time I cleared the tanker. This time I stabilized well clear of the KB-50; far enough back I could see Lead smoothly disconnecting on the other side.

Lead suggested trading places, he'd take the right wing and I'd take the left. I really wanted the flight and this night to be over, nonetheless, I acknowledged his call with an affirmative and we traded positions.

I was physically spent with all the stress. I didn't understand what was happening. I didn't have that many mid-air refuelings under my belt, but what I did have, had never given me trouble and I had enjoyed the experiences of mid-air refuelings.

I successfully hooked up and got my fuel using the left station. The whole time I was refueling, my whole right arm from hand to shoulder ached as I had a death grip on the control stick.

I was surprised nothing much was said about my terrible display of airmanship on the tanker during the flight debrief. But Lead certainly must have said something to the Squadron Ops Officer because I found myself on the schedule again for another mid-air refueling the next night, in an "F" with Capt. Don Woske, the Ops Officer, in my rear seat!

The stress I felt on this flight started way before we ever got close to the tanker; it started as we walked out to the aircraft. I knew I was under the gun. Was I going to be too dangerous to be in the squadron? I never felt this kind of pressure, not even during pilot training in Air Training Command!

We took off at dusk, flew a round robin (navigation flight in the local area, starting and ending at the same location) and then proceeded to the air-refueling track. I flew the plane the entire time; Woske was so silent in the rear seat he made me feel like I was alone in a "D". I was number two again so when we rendezvoused with the tanker, I got that dreaded right wing position! I was cleared into the pre-contact position and I went through the procedures of the night before. Once again, I hooked up on my first attempt, and pushed the hose into the refueling position. I was steady as a rock but could feel my hand tightening up. I kept thinking, come on hurry up; get my fuel before those damn oscillations start again. Finally, the scanner informed me I had received my fuel and that I was cleared to disconnect. What a relief! After disconnecting, Woske finally said, "Let me do one", as he shook the stick indicating he was taking control of the aircraft. It felt so good to just sit there, relaxed and watching him refuel from the back seat.

After getting his fuel, Woske backed off, disconnected from the basket, shook the stick, and said, "You have the airplane". As I acknowledged verbally while simultaneously shaking the stick, Woske said, "Okay, now go refuel off the left wing". Rats! I thought I was done. At least last night I didn't have any trouble refueling on the left wing, I hoped it would be the same that night.

I maneuvered to the left wing pre-contact position, waited for contact clearance, and proceeded to smoothly and effectively refuel off the left pod once I was cleared. Backing off after getting my fuel, I felt more relieved and that I had redeemed myself. But Woske said, "Alright, show me the tail position". Wait a minute, I've never refueled from there before, I felt like saying! But I didn't dare; instead, I moved to the tail pre-contact position and waited for contact clearance. Once again, after getting clearance, I plugged into the tail basket, pushed forward to the refueling position, and got my fuel. I was surprised by how easy the tail position was and by now, I felt like my old self, very confident in my ability to mid-air refuel.

We completed the flight very much like we had started with Woske not saying much for the rest of the mission. I must of have neutralized any bad effects or stigma of the previous night's performance because it wasn't mentioned during the flight debriefing; it was like it had never happened. Although it turned out to be a one-time experience for me in my 24-year career and 100 plus aerial refuelings, this type of incident was not an isolated event.

Two years later, flying F-105s in Japan, I joined up at night on a KB-50's refueling a couple of Thuds. The pilot in the 105 hooked up in the tail drogue was Chan McInelly, a good friend and fellow squadron mate. Waiting my turn, I was watching his plane and noticed his horizontal stabilizer gradually increase its rate and magnitude of movement. I immediately recalled my experience in the F-100 and thought, "Oh my God, Chan, you're going to get into a hellacious "JC". I no sooner thought that and the plane started pitching up and down into ever increasing oscillations as he tried to back off and disconnect from the basket. Having experienced this only two years earlier, I had great empathy for what he was going through but I couldn't resist it and I keyed the mic button and called out, "Ride 'em cowboy!"

While on this deployment, we had to evacuate all our aircraft to Korea when Okinawa was threatened by a typhoon. This provided me a limited opportunity to see and experience more of the Far East. We flew our airplanes in separate flights to Osan AB, Republic of Korea and spent a few days there waiting for the typhoon to pass. When we were cleared to return, our squadron commander, Lt. Col. "Gabby" Reynolds, a World War II P-51 Mustang fighter pilot, decided he wanted to lead all 24 planes back for a mass squadron fly-by at Kadena. The Colonel was a good pilot but getting a little long in the tooth. Some of the younger pilots questioned the wisdom of this plan but he was the boss and no one was going to tell him we shouldn't do it. He briefed we would pass over the field at pattern altitude, six flights of four in trail, go back out over the ocean, split up the mass formation into our individual flights and reenter the pattern for VFR pitch outs and landings. Simple plan, what could possibly go wrong?

The flight from Osan to the letdown point for entry to the initial at Kadena went as briefed. I was in the back seat of an "F" in the fourth flight in the string of six. I had my mirrors on the canopy bow adjusted so I could see the flights behind us as long as they were in good position. Approaching the turn to initial, "Gabby" overshot it and had to continue the turn to correct back and then reverse his turn to line up with initial. This produced a corkscrew effect on the 24 plane formation where the first few flights were in a right bank turn while the trailing flights were in a left bank turn. It got kind of hairy for the trailing flights and suddenly, in the mirrors, I spotted three wingmen, two in the flight directly behind us, and one in the last flight, break out of formation! Someone up front radioed, "You okay back there?" The fly-by certainly wasn't the prettiest ever seen by Kadena!

My anxiety to get home increased the closer we got to the end of our three month rotation. Even though my first deployment had been a great experience with a lot of good flying and exposure to a part of the world new to me, it had been hard being separated this long from my family. My two young sons were at ages where kids grow and change immensely in a short period of time and I was missing that. I already had most of my Far East purchases of major items and souvenirs I wanted to bring home, I was ready! Only a few more days and we'd be on the "Freedom Bird" headed for home.

In the dark of night, we awoke in our quarters to the blare of base sirens. Along with my two roommates, I got up still half asleep, put on my flight suit and headed to our squadron operations building. We were all milling around in the main briefing room, some joking, others complaining about being awoken again one more time for a practice alert just before rotating back home. "Gabby" Reynolds rushed into the room and onto the stage, turned to us with a very concerned look on his face and announced, "Gentlemen, this is not a practice alert, this is the real thing!" The room went momentarily silent. Reynolds added we were at DEFCON 3 (Highest level of Defense Condition ever reached by tactical forces in post war era - Strategic Air Command went to DEFCON 2)

It was 22 October 1962, the first hour of the "Cuban Missile Crisis". We were told we would be assigned to planes being uploaded with nuclear weapons to augment those already on the nuclear alert pad. The look on some of my friends' faces was beyond worried, it was terrifying! A few guys were scrambling for something to write on; they wanted to write a "last message" home. I thought this was crazy. If we did launch, did they really think there was going to be a surviving postal service? This was Armageddon!

We remained in the briefing room the rest of the night, waiting for assignments to the additional nuclear loaded aircraft, which never occurred. As the hours passed, things appeared to simmer down. We were able to hear President Kennedy's speech to the nation. Finally, in the early morning hours, we were allowed to go back to our rooms and get some sleep with instructions to be ready to report on a moment's notice. This was one of my scariest moments in my career. I really thought we were about to go to war with nukes!

The squadron soon received a higher headquarters message stating our redeployment back to Homestead was delayed a week. A week later we received a similar message that now pushed our return home into November. Meanwhile I'm writing home giving my wife the disappointing news. The weekly delays continued into December when the final message changed from "delayed a week" to "delayed indefinitely." We couldn't understand why we were still being held over in Okinawa, the Cuban Missile Crisis had subsided in November and the nation was back to DEFCON 5 normalcy. The one good thing coming out of this was we were getting a lot of good flying hours. I added 42 hours and 25 minutes to my F-100 experience during the period we were extended past our scheduled return.

Our three-month deployment had already gone on for five months! The extension had a detrimental effect on squadron morale, especially when we received the last message stating we were extended indefinitely and it looked like we would miss the holidays with our families. Before receipt of the "indefinitely delayed" message, I thought we'd be home for Christmas and had written my wife earlier not to bother getting any toys, explaining there were lots of neat battery operated Japanese toys I'd bring home for Christmas. Now with this latest notification, I had to break the bad news I wouldn't be home for the holidays and that she should get the kids' presents after all.

Before Christmas, the squadron received another one of those messages we had developed a genuine dislike for, but this one was different, we were notified we were rotating home and we would return by 22 December. I quickly went into town and stocked up on a bunch of toys for my sons. Meanwhile, my wife had bought a collection of toys based on my previous letter saying I wasn't going to make it home for Christmas and for her to buy the boys' presents. Needless to say, Christmas 1962 was one of the best Christmases for the little Munchkins, my wife and myself!

Chapter 4: Donald Duck Becomes a Night Owl

The 309th's primary mission changed in early 1963 when we became the 31st TFW's Night Owl Squadron. This meant the squadron would be doing a lot more flying at night, including night weapons delivery. Hurling yourself at the ground in day time can be fun and exciting in an F-100 but I suspected at night, it would be more exciting than fun!

A three-phased graduated training program was created to qualify everyone in the squadron in various night events. The first two phases consisted of single ship 200-foot low-level night navigation training missions. In phase one, the training program started out easy using brightly lit towns and cities as waypoints; it was so simple, you could see the glow of the next brightly lit turning point miles away on the horizon. At the completion of the route, we'd climb and return to Homestead at 15,000 to 17,000 feet. After flying a specified number of these courses, we progressed to phase two and flew more challenging missions where the waypoints were unlit rural road intersections or a shack barely lit on the edge of some swamp. The third phase was to qualify in night weapons delivery under the light of illuminating flares.

Capt. Jack Gilchrist briefed the night's missions even though he was in the final phase while I was about half way through phase two. He checked the timing and location of when I'd finish my route and he selected a circuit from phase one that would put us in the vicinity of each other near the same time. He briefed I could join up with him over Orlando, follow him and orbit over the range while he dropped his bombs, and then he would lead me back to Homestead.

I flew my course, thankful for a sliver of moonlight, which made it a little easier to spot some of the more obscured waypoints. I completed my route on time and hopped on over to brightly lit Orlando, checking with Jack on his location. Just as he radioed that he was directly over the city, I spotted him a couple thousand feet beneath me in a left turn. I called out "Tally-Ho" and started descending to join up. The normal procedure for a turning join up is to approach the aircraft you are joining from the inside of the turn. Unfortunately, when I first spotted him, I was to the outside of his turn and even though I was trying to get to the inside, I was still approaching from the outside.

Jack had gone bright steady on his navigation lights approaching Orlando to help me get a tally. The navigation light directly behind the cockpit was a clear light that reflected into the cockpit when in the bright position. As I was still trying to close on him from above, Jack asked me to let him know when he could go back to dim steady on his lights, as he was getting a lot of glare from the light directly behind the canopy. Being the hotshot young tiger I thought I was, I cleared him to go dim steady immediately. Shockingly, when he did, all his lights except the light behind the canopy went out. His plane was still silhouetted against the brilliant lights of the city below as I continued descending from above and outside of the turn. The single light should have been an alarm bell but the clear view of Jack's plane against the city lights gave me a false sense that I could complete the join up so I didn't say anything about his lights being out in the dim steady position.

As I closed in on the join up, instead of the visual cues improving, they got drastically worse. The contour of the F-100 suddenly disappeared as it blended in with the night when I descended to its level and lost the city background lighting. Now I was just joining up on a single light against a solid black backdrop. All of a sudden, my left windshield panel was full of F-100! I yanked back on the control stick and felt slight turbulence as I went over the top of him. "I think you just hit me!" was the first thing I heard over the radio! I immediately came back with, "Are you all right?" Before Jack could answer, a new voice came over the radio, "Who hit who?" it was the recognizable voice of our commander, "Gabby" Reynolds who was also up flying that night. Jack using our call sign said, "I think two just hit me."

Reynolds didn't inquire how our planes were flying nor had any idea of our condition, yet he instructed me to join up with Jack and check him over for damage! I couldn't believe it; joining up on a guy I just hit, that was the last thing I wanted to do. Obviously, Jack had similar feelings about having a guy who just hit him make another pass at him because he immediately answered Reynolds with, "No, that's all right. I have it under control." But Reynolds insisted I join up and look Jack over.

I tried to locate Jack but I think he had poured the coals to it in an attempt to make sure I didn't get near him. I knew he was somewhere out in front of me and at a higher altitude. Every once in a while we would give each other TACAN radial cuts and mileage as if we were still trying to join up. It was evident there was no way I would catch him before he reached Homestead.

When I landed, they parked me right next to Jack's plane that was all lit up by mobile ramp lighting equipment. As my engine wound down after

I shut down, I examined Jack's plane from my cockpit as I unstrapped. I couldn't see any damage and asked the crew chief who had rushed up my ladder, if I had hit him. As he got level with me in the cockpit, he turned towards Jack's plane and pointing to the tail said, "Check the antenna on the top of the tail". The F-100 had a small antenna about six inches tall above the top of the vertical stabilizer. Jack's was bent 90 degrees to the left.

As close as one can come to a mid-air collision without colliding! Small Antenna on Top of Tail Got bent 90 Degrees From Near Mid-Air Collision.

(Personal Photo)

As I was climbing down the ladder, I heard the crew chief from underneath my plane exclaim, "Found it". He had located a nice clean white streak where dirt had been scraped off across the bottom of the dirty SUU-21 bomb dispenser on the centerline station of my F-100. This is the closest contact one can have between two aircraft without having a mid-air collision!

I survived the incident, the squadron chalking it up as another learning experience in the maturation of a fighter pilot. But the incident did not pass without consequences. The squadron decided that one needed at least 800 hours flying experience to be in the Night Owl program. All the young pilots with less than 800 hours were exchanged with more experienced pilots in other squadrons. I was reassigned to the 307th TFS.

This reshuffling of Lieutenants had unintended consequences and did not last very long. The 309th had become rank heavy with an unbalanced rank structure. The older officers complained about being assigned to menial tasks usually performed by junior officers.

About two months later, Lt. Col. Sullivan, the 307th commander, informed me that all the Lieutenants who had come out of the 309th were going to be transferred back. He said he'd like me to stay in his squadron and could arrange it if I wanted it. I felt I fit well in the 307th so I thanked him and agreed to stay.

Although it had been several months since the Cuban Missile Crisis, the Wing still kept two birds cocked by the end of the runway on Air Defense alert status. Alert duty on weekends was kind of boring with very little activity on the ramp. At least during the week, the time went by much faster watching base F-100s and B-52s taking off and landing. I experienced my first alert launch on a weekend when Lou Batson and I got scrambled and were given vectors to an unidentified bogey inbound towards the base from the direction of Cuba. It was exciting and I had visions of possibly encountering a defecting MiG pilot. Instead, while still climbing and not too far from Homestead, I got an engine low oil pressure caution light. The F-100 had a propensity for bad oil gauge transducers but you still had to treat it as a valid indication even when it was a suspected malfunctioning gauge. If it was an actual oil malfunction and you lost all oil pressure, you only had 10 to 30 minutes to get on the ground before the engine would seize.

I informed Lou of my situation, declared an emergency, and my intention to recover from a Simulated Flame Out (SFO) pattern. He acknowledged, said he would fly safety chase and follow me back to Homestead.

I approached high key and called Homestead tower requesting an SFO pattern (High key is a point 10,000 feet over the intended landing, flying a 360 degree SFO pattern). I reached high key a little high so I extended the cross wind and hit the low key in better shape but still slightly high (5,200 feet versus desired 5,000 feet). Meanwhile, Lou had been chasing me in the pattern without saying a word. Turning final, I was still a little high but I felt I was in good shape with plenty of runway ahead of me.

I'd rather land long than be short with a frozen engine if it failed on me. Then an authoritative voice came over the radio, the call sign of the Wing Commander saying, "F-100 on final, take it around"!

I momentarily hesitated in making a decision, do I continue on with what looks like a good approach, or do I follow the Wing Commander's order and advance the power for a go-around and chance freezing up the engine? A little pissed at having to make the choice, I gingerly advanced the throttle and executed a go round while requesting a closed pattern (Climbing turn to downwind for an immediate landing rather than leaving the airfield pattern and going out to reenter at initial and start a new overhead pattern).

Receiving tower clearance for the closed pattern, I pulled up to downwind with landing gear and flaps still extended, gritting my teeth as I flew the landing pattern to touch down; the oil pressure gauge had read zero pressure ever since reaching high key.

Safely on the ground, I felt more confident that it was only the gauge so rather than shutting down after clearing the runway and having to be towed, I taxied to my parking spot a short distance away. Col. Frank "Spot" Collins, our Wing Commander was leaning against his staff car, arms crossed over his chest, along with the Wing Flying Safety Officer standing right next to him as I turned into my parking spot. The Wing Flying Safety Officer's pick up was on the other side of the Colonel's staff car. My angry mood quickly changed to worry of how much trouble I might be in being met by this high power greeting party!

I climbed down the ladder and saluted Colonel Collins. He returned the salute and immediately told me he wanted me in his office at 09:00, Monday morning, ready to explain why I couldn't fly a proper SFO! I acknowledged and saluted as he turned, opened the door to his staff car, got in and drove off.

I looked perplexed at the Flying Safety Captain. He started in on me, "Vic, I wouldn't of gone around for all the tea in China! Never let anyone else fly your airplane, especially from the ground, no matter who it is! Your approach and pattern were fine. Don't worry about it. Don't show up Monday morning. I'll go for you instead and take care of it!" At about that time, Lou walked up asking what the hell was going on? The Wing Safety officer explained that Collins wasn't even on the flight line when he instructed me to go around; that he was driving towards the ramp observing from his staff car and there was no way he could have had proper perspective of my pattern. Lou piped in agreement saying that my SFO pattern was just fine. The Safety officer assured us that he would take care of the matter and not to worry about it.

On Sunday, even though I had the backing of the Safety officer and my flight Lead, I still worried all day about not showing up the next morning at Colonel Collins' office as ordered. But I did as the Safety Officer had instructed me and on Monday morning I instead went over to maintenance and checked whether the engine really was losing oil pressure or was it a bad transducer. As suspected, it was just a bad gauge transducer. Mid-morning, I received a call from the Wing Safety officer telling me he had taken care of the matter with Collins and not to worry about it, it was all over. I thanked him but before he let me go, he reminded me one more time that the pilot in the cockpit was ultimately the only one in command of the aircraft. It was good sound advice and one I carried with me the rest of my career.

In May, the 307th deployed to McCord AFB, Tacoma, Washington, to participate as part of the Red Force in a war game exercise code name Coulee Crest. This was my first major war game exercise in my career. It may have been my imagination but the F-100 appeared to operate much better in the cooler dry Washington air than Florida's. We comfortably operated at 36,000 feet, an altitude we seldom flew at around Florida. We flew a variety of missions, road recce, ground attack, and air-to-air.

The biggest exercise challenge was differentiating between Red and Blue forces as both sides were operating similar equipment. Even when the forces were dissimilar, it was still hard to know who was who. In one of the earliest missions, I was flying as number four in a simulated armed road recce mission, weaving back and forth over a major road at 500 feet. I would regularly check our six o'clock to make sure it was still clear. During one of these checks, I spotted a single RF-101 at our four-thirty position, also weaving back and forth over a road parallel with our road. This unusual maneuvering for an RF-101 threw me, I couldn't understand why it would be doing the same mission so close to where we were. This made me suspect it was from the opposing force and I called him out as a bogey. I didn't have enough lateral separation so I started an outside circling turn to engage him but my element Lead called me off and told me to rejoin the flight. Since I had already started the turn I just continued the 360 and got a better look at the One O' Wonder as I pushed it up and went by him to rejoin my flight.

There is an old saying in the fighter pilot world, "If you ain't cheating, you ain't trying". To enhance our air-to-air advantage over Blue forces,

Lt. Col. Sullivan ordered maintenance to download the external tanks on about half of our birds. It was a rarity to fly a clean bird back at the home base so this was a pleasurable opportunity, especially when fighting an F-100 loaded down with external wing tanks. With the exception of a few hotshot pilots, most Blue F-100's would try to avoid getting into a turning dogfight with us when we were clean. They would only make slashing high-speed passes if the opportunity presented itself. I achieved a gun camera kill on a Blue force F-100 as he tried to separate from me.

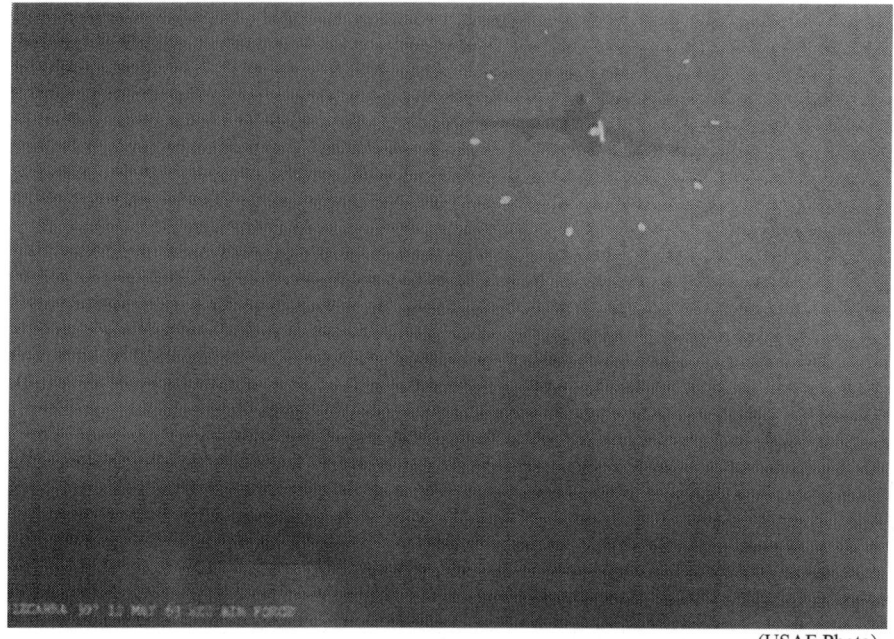

(USAF Photo)
Author's Gun Camera Confirms "Air Kill" of Blue F-100.

Learning that an upcoming target was a Blue Army bivouac area, I came up with an idea of drawing a propaganda leaflet to drop on Blue ground forces. I drew a sexy female with a garrison cap, blouse partially unbuttoned, a lot of leg showing because her skirt was partially hiked to her thigh from the way she was sitting. The leaflet invited Blue forces to put down their arms and join her in a better life on the Red side. We mimeographed a bunch of copies for the mission and stuffed them into the speed brake well.

We took off and headed for our Blue Army bivouac target to deliver the "goods", mindful of not being able to use the speed brake like my earlier days at Homestead. We dove in on the camp area and simulated a strafing attack; passing over the line of tents, I extended the speed brake, spreading the leaflets over the tents. We only made one pass so I didn't

(USAF Photo)

Author's Gun Camera Records "Dry Strafe" of Blue Bivouac Area.

get a chance to see the results of our tomfoolery on the Blue ground troops.

After the mission, one of our squadron pilots got a call from a friend serving as the Blue Air Liaison Officer (ALO). I could only hear the conversation at our end of the phone call but from my squadron mate's responses, it was obvious he was asking who drew the flier? My squadron mate, not sure where the questioning was heading, cautiously told him it was one of the guys in the squadron. The ALO's comment must of have been very complimentary because my buddy on the phone turned and looked at me with a big smile and a thumbs up while saying, "Yes, he is quite talented". When he got off the phone he told me his buddy said the Blue ground troops thought the flier was great! It was a fun exercise.

About two months later, I was notified I would be receiving orders to F-105's in Japan. I went home for lunch and told the wife the news. She called Pat Stamps and told her about our future assignment. While still on the phone with my Pat, Pat Stamps told her husband, Jerry, "The Vizcarra's just got orders to Japan in 105's". Since we had been with the Stamps from the start of our Air Force careers, Jerry said, "I better go back to the squadron and check if we got orders".... And they had!

On August, 1963, I flew what I thought was my last F-100 flight and departed Homestead AFB for Nellis AFB to check out in the F-105D. A few weeks later, I received notice from the 307th TFS, my F-100 squadron, that there was an error and I was short one flight to meet my proportionate share of AFM 60-1 requirements for a Permanent Change of Station (PCS). They were going to fly an F-100F out to Nellis so I could get that last required flight. I had already started F-105 academics but had not yet started flying the F-105.

Capt. Don Woske, my old 309th TFS Ops Officer, showed up for my "new" last F-100 flight. I hopped in the back seat and off we went. Don was very quiet, never saying much when flying, but I respected him, he was a great officer and pilot. He never offered me any stick time, it seemed like I was just along for the ride filling the AFM 60-1 square. I finally just rested my arms along the canopy seal so he could see them in his mirrors thinking that might give him a hint and offer me some stick time. My arms were still on the seals when Don entered initial for the landing. His pitch out was so sudden and sharp, it bounced my head off the side of the canopy, a real surprise. He flew the tightest F-100 pattern I'd ever seen. I was positive anyone watching from the ground would think I was showing off flying a shit hot tight pattern!

On the ground, I got a smile out of his usual serious look when I said, "Nice pattern"! He knew I was referring to his bouncing my head off the canopy, I saw him looking at me in the mirrors when he did it. He responded with an extended arm to shake my hand thanking me and wishing me luck in the F-105.

Although my final F-100 assignment was to the 307th, I still felt a certain affinity to my first operational squadron, the 309th. Unknown to me, I had left a part of me that would stay with the squadron decades after I was gone. While assigned to the 309th, I had painted what became known as the "Duck Board", a 4 by 6 foot board with the two hemispheres of the world, Donald Duck, dressed in the local attire, superimposed over that part of the globe where the squadron had deployed. In the center of the board was a list of the types of aircraft and years flown by the squadron starting with the P-39 during World War II and a list of the Squadron Commanders and the dates of their command.

Nineteen years after leaving Homestead, I returned as an O-6 (Full Colonel) to check out in the F-4. It was a nostalgic time for me; my old squadron, the 307th was now minimally manned with only a few instructors who checked out pilots in a short training course. The squadron did not even have any assigned aircraft and had to use the other squadrons' aircraft.

For my scheduled first flight, after briefing in the 307th, my instructor and I walked across the street to my other old squadron building, the 309th to get an assigned aircraft. As we entered the building, I was shocked and surprised to see my "Duck Board" still hanging on the wall across from the ops desk and scheduling board. I guess the Squadron Commander had been informed there was a student O-6 scheduled to fly one of his planes because he was waiting for my entrance and he called the building to attention as I entered. He extended his hand in welcome but all I could do was stare at the "Duck Board" saying, "Oh my God, it is still here, I painted that when I was a Lieutenant in the squadron in 1963"! I think the Squadron Commander was now as shocked as I was as he leaned close to the board looking for my signature asking where it was when he couldn't find it. I told him I had never signed it. Without hesitation, he turned to a Lieutenant in the squadron and told him to go get a can of yellow paint (squadron color) and a small brush and told me I needed to sign the board! The display had been kept current since my departure nineteen years earlier.

Two decades later, I was informed the "Duck Board" was still in being and now hung in the lobby of the Officers' Club at Luke AFB, AZ. I don't know if that was correct, but sure would be a nice legacy if it were.

The flight with Woske put me at 448 hours of F-100C/D/F flying time, closing out what I thought was to be my chapter in flying the F-100. A difficult aircraft to fly correctly, I believed I had mastered its idiosyncrasies and was a better pilot for it. I may have believed that but as far as the Air Force was concerned, I wasn't quite there yet. An Air Force study had determined pilots with less than 800 hours had the highest risk of being involved in a flight accident. My total military flying experience was 740 hours.

Chapter 5: Edwards Air Force Flight Test Center

After leaving the F-100, I spent three and a half years in Japan flying the F-105. I was gone from home an awful lot, nuclear alert in Korea, three TDY combat tours to Southeast Asia including an ejection and rescue over North Vietnam, ferrying aircraft to the combat zone and Taiwan overhaul depot, range officer etc. etc. The family needed a rest from all these separations. My wife, with just cause, asked me to seek an assignment more conducive to family life. This meant I needed to get out of the tactical environment. On a TDY to the states, I stopped by Randolph AFB Personnel Assignments and spoke with an Assignments Officer. He must have taken pity on me because after seeing him, our assignment out of Japan was to Air Force Systems Command, Air Force Flight Test Center (AFFTC), Edwards AFB, California, two hours from home.

While stationed at Edwards, I was fortunate to witness some historical flights, the late '60s were interesting and exciting times at this test Mecca. Five months after our getting stationed there, Pete Knight set a speed record of Mach 6.72 (4,520 mph) at 102,100 feet in the X-15, a record that still remains in 2017. The X-15 pilots were real pioneers in hypersonic-rocket powered flight, testing the edge of outer space.

My flying assignment at Edwards initially was anti-climatic after flying the F-105, but it did relieve the constant family separations associated with Tactical Air Command. I was assigned to AFFTC Headquarters Plans and Programs Office as a Plans officer (boring) and to Base Operations flying the T-33.

I tried to work my way into flying with the Flight Test Operations Division but was told I wasn't qualified since I was not a graduate of the Center's Test Pilot School. Disappointed, I would bide my time, figuring the day would come when they would need me regardless of not being a "Golden Arm" (test pilot school graduate)!

Base Operations welcomed me with open arms. They needed someone who loved to fly and sought flying time at every opportunity; that was me. I rapidly earned a reputation for always being available to take a flight regardless of time or day. I was quickly designated a senior Stan/Eval check pilot, instructor pilot (IP), and Functional Check Flight (FCF) pilot. It didn't take me long to realize that flying the T-33 in these capacities was much more enjoyable than flying it as a student pilot. I wasn't particularly fond of it while going through pilot training.

I got extremely proficient in the T-33, successfully completing SFO landings from inordinate distances and altitudes. Another pilot and I would also fly overhead patterns, set the throttle just prior to pitching out and see who could touch down closest to the runway numbers without touching the throttle. We both got quite good at cross controlling the rudder and ailerons, causing the aircraft to slip and rapidly lose altitude to touch down at the aiming spot on the runway.

Before long, my reputation made its way back to the Flight Test Operations Division. The Vietnam War was coming up on its fourth year since the Gulf of Tonkin incident; the Division was ripe with candidates who had not yet been to Southeast Asia and were starting to get assignments to the war. They invited me to start flying with them on safety chase and photo support missions.

My first major test program was flying safety chase during C-5 stall tests in late 1968. I marveled watching this monstrosity of an aircraft increase its angle of attack until it stalled and the nose dropped to gain speed and recover.

I was getting a lot of enjoyable flying time but the fact that I came home from Japan 41 missions short of a combat tour was hanging over my head. The war had heated up and I knew I would eventually need to go back to Southeast Asia. I discussed this with my wife and broached the idea of possibly volunteering to go back but Pat wasn't too happy about the prospect of me returning to combat. We had barely had a year of family stability with minimal separations at Edwards.

Several of the Air Force personal we socialized with were enrolling in an on base evening Master's degree program. Pat suggested I consider doing that instead of volunteering for Southeast Asia, pointing out it was not only an educational opportunity but also at least another year of a stable home life. When she added she could then support me volunteering if I must, I thought it was a good compromise so I enrolled in the Master's program.

In December 1968, Edwards received a message seeking volunteers to ferry two T-33's to Brazil. Other than the fact that it was just before the holidays, I found the request appealing. After coordinating with the home "Chief of Staff", I and two other Edward pilots, Gary and "Smoky" volunteered. Guess there weren't too many volunteers interested in being gone so close to Christmas because the three of us from Edwards were selected for the mission along with a Major from Air Training Command (ATC).

When it came time to team up, I was the odd man out since Gary and "Smoky" were close friends and worked in the same department; so I ended being crewed with the ATC Major. We picked up the airplanes at the Melbourne Maintenance Depot in Florida and flew them to Kelly AFB, Texas, with the Major in the front seat.

The next day, I took the front seat and started us out towards Mexico City, our next stop. I was surprised when we crossed into Mexican airspace and traveled out of radio range of the US Centers, it became impossible to raise the Mexican Centers and give position reports. This started a periodic but frequent instruction from the Major in the back seat telling me what I needed to do. It was evident that he was in his instructor pilot mode and I was his student -- irritating! I quickly learned all I needed to do to stop his incessant instruction was to acknowledge his communiqué but ignore his instruction and keep flying the way I wanted.

Upon landing at Mexico International Airport, the airplane veered left when I started applying the wheel brakes; we had lost our right brake! Luckily, we still had enough speed and rudder control to straighten the aircraft on the centerline. The Major asked what was going on at the same time I started explaining we had no right wheel brake. Suddenly, the plane veered left again and I asked what the hell was going on. He replied he was just checking the brakes to which I angrily blurted out "Knock it off!"

I straightened the plane out again, barely keeping it on the runway, still rolling fairly fast and very close to the left edge of the runway. I simultaneously informed the tower of our situation as I raised the large canopy trying to use it as a speed brake. Meanwhile, the Major is nervously asking if we are going to be able to stop before running out of runway. I wasn't sure we could stop in time as I could see the overrun quickly approaching. I stop-cocked the throttle shutting down the engine just in case, it helped and it looked like we were going to be able to stop before reaching the overrun.

I informed the tower I had shut off the engine to ensure we didn't go off the end of the runway. They requested if there was any way to taxi off the runway to please do so as they had an American Airlines 707 three miles out on final. As they were finishing their transmission, I heard and felt a rumble and saw the engine exhaust gauge temperature rapidly rising and approaching an over temp condition. I yelled, "What are you doing?" He replied he was trying to get the engine started for me. For a second time within minutes I had to tell him to "Knock it off."

By the time the event was all over and we had been towed off the runway, I was really pissed. Mindful of the excellent advice given me by the Wing Safety Officer at Homestead five years prior about being in command of your own aircraft, I pulled the Major aside and as tactfully as a Captain can chew out a Major, I informed him there can only be one pilot in command and that for this trip, it would be the pilot in the front seat. I think my brashness surprised him because he was momentarily lost for words. He finally just shook his head as if he understood.

After we got that sorted out, I went about trying to get the wheel brake repaired. I was confident there wouldn't be any problem with being fluent in Spanish, and the Mexican Air Force having T-33's stationed on the military side of the airport. Guess my fluency in the language wasn't as good as I thought because when the mechanic showed up I couldn't make it clear to him that the right wheel brake needed repairing. Finally resorting to pig Latin, sign language, and lots of pointing the light came on. Turns out the word I was using for brake wasn't the local dialect.

When he finished the repair, I asked what we owed him and he nodded nothing. I empathized for him; it was obvious he wasn't getting paid much. His T-shirt was pretty tattered and worn out. We already had our garment bags out from the nose of the T-33 so I reached in my bag and pulled out one of my new T-shirts and handed it to him. His eyes lit up and he got the happiest grin on his face. Raising his hand with the T-shirt as if he was toasting me, he said "Muchos Gracias!"

The next morning we started off on the next leg of the trip to Howard AB, Panama Canal Zone with a refueling stop on the way in Guatemala City. With the Major in the front seat, the communications between cockpits was much more amicable than the day before.

My turn in the front seat, we took-off the next day headed for Caracas, Venezuela, shocked to find I had the old Major in the back again; Vic check your speed, you need to turn to heading so and so, watch your altitude, etc. etc. It was so bad; I had to just mentally block him out of my mind. It would be terrible to not hear him in an emergency!

When we landed in Caracas, we were chocked with a rock. I felt bad to think that when we picked up the airplane at Melbourne, it looked like it had just come off the production line, and here a little over half way to its destination, the engine had already been over temped once and now chocked with a rock!

By now, I had shared my frustration about the Major with Gary and "Smokey". They were not surprised and had an inclination of what he was like from our social evenings together.

Preparing for our departure from Caracas, we got concerned when the Venezuelan who was going to launch us showed up with a lower amp power unit than we needed. We asked for a larger unit but were told this was all that was available. It was the Major's turn in the front seat. We talked about monitoring the engine temp carefully because of the power unit we were using and to abort the engine start if the temperature started approaching starting limits. After discussing these precautions, the Major continued with the engine start in spite of over temping the engine, albeit, not as bad as when he tried to restart the engine in Mexico City! This leg took us to Suriname for another over night stay.

During this entire trip, we had flown each leg individually, usually with five-minute separation in take-off times. From Suriname, it was just two hops to our final destination, Recife. We decided that we would meet up at the next field where we would refuel and then would fly in formation with me leading us in a low approach over Recife for a tactical pitch up to the landing pattern. French Guiana would not grant over flight clearance so leaving Suriname, we had to circumnavigate out over the Atlantic clear of French Guiana. The other T-bird departed first; we followed a few minutes later with me in command in the front seat. As part of the climb check passing through 2,000 feet, I check the wing fuel tanks for siphoning and damn we had fuel siphoning out of our left leading edge wing fuel cap! I cussed while telling the Major in the back we had fuel siphoning, he said, "We have to go back and land.!" I said, no, watch this as I altered course and took us over French Guiana direct towards our next refueling stop. The Major got all excited saying we couldn't do this. I told him we haven't talked to any center between departing and arriving control towers since leaving the US; nobody even knows we are there in transit! For good measure, I added, even if French Guiana knows we are here, what are they going to do, send a couple of Corsairs to intercept us? For the first time since leaving the US, he was silent while I flew the bird!

Taking the short cut, we beat the other T-bird and landed first even though they had taken off five minutes before us. Gary asked how we had gotten there first and just grinned when I told him and "Smoky" what I had done. We re-briefed the approach and our entry into the landing pattern using a tactical pitch up to make sure we all understood what we were going to do upon our arrival at Recife and then headed out to our planes.

Once airborne, the old Major was back again instructing me on how to lead the formation; guess you can't take the instructor pilot out of a pilot who has spent his whole career in Training Command.

I got concerned over the ever-increasing cloud cover as we approached Recife and began wondering if we would be able to execute our planned tactical pitch. I rocked my wings signaling Gary to get in close formation and started to pick our way through holes in the clouds all while hearing a constant yakety yak from the rear seat! Spotting a large hole and Recife off in the far distance, I looked over at Gary and gave him the throttling back hand signal as I pushed over and dove through the hole.

Once underneath the cloud ceiling, the visibility was great and we approached the airfield 100 feet above the flat terrain. I kept checking Gary's position on my right wing; he was in nice and tight as if he were a "Thunderbird". We screamed in over the runway and at mid-field I pitched up and rolled into a tight turn onto the downwind leg of the landing pattern. Gary followed suit three seconds later; a great conclusion to a six day trip.

After the flight, "Smoky" told me when we leveled off at 100 feet, the Major in my back seat must have thought they were too low and kept looking at them gesturing with his hands for them to stack higher in the formation. "Smoky" said he finally had enough and gave him the finger. It was hard to take the Major seriously!

Even though I was only gone a week, I had missed the mid-term exam in my Master's program and hadn't even started my term paper which was due in a week. I decided I had gotten too far behind the course to catch up so I went to the Base Education Office to disenroll. Dr. Rose, the USC professor for my class happened to be in the office and was surprised to see me. He said I had been missed and asked where I had been. When I told him of my trip to Brazil and that I was there to disenroll because I was too far behind, he disagreed. He encouraged and talked me into remaining in the program. His personal interest, encouragement, and sound advice were a major event in my life for which I am eternally grateful.

Contrary to many headquarters, AFFTC was not inundated with lots of long hours of staff work and last minute deadlines. This gave me great flexibility in being able to fly even on short notice. One Thursday, I received a call in my office at quitting time from base operations asking if I could start a quick jet recurrency training of a pilot the next day that would carry over into the weekend. I was starting to get annoyed by these constant last minute requests, but I had created a reputation of never saying "no". My last year at Edwards, I began saying "Check and see if you can get someone else, if you can't find anyone, call me back". I'd always get a call back!

My new "student" was a pilot who had just received orders to check out in the F-4 for an assignment to Southeast Asia. But it had been so many years since he had flown a jet, higher headquarters wanted him requalified in a jet with a certain amount of hours before reporting to the F-4 schoolhouse. The only way we could accumulate the needed number of hours in a short period was to include a long cross-country over the weekend.

On Friday, we flew two transition sorties with him in the front seat doing air work and lots of patterns and landings. The next day we met at Base Ops and filed a cross-country to Webb AFB, Texas with him in the back under the hood (a sheath that covers the rear canopy so the pilot can not see out) for an extended instrument flight. I planned to swap seats with him to get him nighttime during the return flight late that evening. The flight to Webb progressed normally until I started having intermittent radio transmission problems that got worse as we approached our letdown point. I had him come out from under the hood; he had been doing fine flying instruments. I told him that I could still hear him on intercom and outside radio transmissions, but that he was going to have to take over transmitting all further radio calls.

When he called the tower, they provided the field weather condition which included an advisory of a developing dust storm west of the field headed their way, that they were only accepting straight in approaches and transferred us to GCA for landing. The crosswind component was only a couple of knots below maximum for the T-Bird but what got my attention was the occasional gust which exceeded the max allowable!

The visibility was terrible with the blowing dust turning the entire outside brown. As we started the GCA, my trainee told me to just take control of the aircraft whenever I acquired the runway; looking at him in the mirror, I acknowledged with a thumbs up. He flew a good GCA but it was evident that the strong crosswind was playing havoc with the runway line-up because when I finally spotted the field, we were right of the runway and lined up with the ramp. I grabbed the stick with a quick shake to let him know I had the airplane and started a missed approach.

When he realized we had missed the runway, he radioed we were going missed approach and requested vectors to another GCA. I followed the vectors given and once we were turned onto a downwind leg, I shook the stick signaling him to take control of the aircraft. Checking him in the mirror again, I saw him acknowledge simultaneously with a head nod and a shake of the control stick.

I hoped I might get a visual a little sooner on this next approach now that I had a better idea of where to search for the field after the first GCA. The second pattern was flown similar to the first, perfect glide slope with constant two to three degree azimuth corrections for line up. As we got closer to touchdown, we were rocked with ever increasing wing wobbles by the crosswind. I spotted the runway, we were lined up with the right edge as I shook the stick, took control and banked left trying to get us over to at least the centerline. We touched down still in a left bank and only on the left main wheel. The airplane felt squirrelly, like it wasn't on the ground and as if it still wanted to fly. As I started to center the stick to get both main wheels on the runway, the left wing started to come up as a gust of wind caught us again and we started drifting towards the right edge of the runway. Under normal circumstances, I would have had the throttle back to idle by now but I felt like I had more control of the aircraft by slowing its speed dissipation with the throttle. I kept us on the runway with full left aileron and rudder. I didn't feel like I had everything under control until all three wheels were on the runway and the air speed was passing through 60-Kts.

The dust storm passed while we flight planned in Base Operations for our return night flight and then had a bite to eat in the cafeteria. My "trainee" complimented me on landing in the dust storm and with such a strong crosswind, he thought it was quite an impressive feat. Oh, if he only knew how scared I was for those first few seconds on the ground, when I was more along for the ride than being in control!

Several months later, I ran into him at the Officer's Club bar. He had flown cross-country into Edwards in an F-4 with his instructor. When he saw me, you would have thought we were long lost friends. He was so excited introducing me to his F-4 instructor, telling him I was the guy who got him jet re-qualified, adding, "You should see this guy land a T-Bird in a dust storm with hellacious crosswinds!" He was having a terrific time, a reborn fighter pilot. I felt bad I didn't stay in touch with him; he was a nice guy and a good pilot. I've often wondered if he survived the war, I hope and pray he did.

In 1969, I was involved flying photo chase on the F-4 spin test project established due to a high incidence of F-4 spin losses. It turned out the Navy had never completed its F-4 spin tests when it lost the modified test aircraft in a spin. Tactical Air Command spin accidents had become a major problem justifying the resurrection of an F-4 spin test project, this time, conducted under the auspices of the Air Force. When the proposed test program was presented to higher headquarters, F-4 spins had become such a sensitive subject; references to spins in the test plan were eliminated and replaced with deep stalls wherever possible.

An F-4E was modified with an oversized spin recovery chute and Major Jerry Gentry of Lifting Body fame was appointed as the project Test Pilot. I flew some of the initial photo chase missions and was told that some of the best film documentation of the tests was acquired when I was the photo chase. Staying in position for the photographer in the back seat to get good stable film required flying smoothly at relative slow speeds. I had to quickly learn where to position our starting point to time it so we'd be almost line abreast with Jerry when he got into his deepest part of the stall. Jerry flew the F-4 to high AOA's and took the stall into where the aircraft would develop a serious wing rock before he would push forward, lower the nose, and break the stall. I'd be about 500 to 800 feet to his right and near stalling speed myself by the end of his maneuver. After conducting several of these deep stalls, we'd return to Edwards at 20,000 feet where he would deploy the spin recovery chute and descend in a steep dive with the spin chute trailing behind him and land. Again, timing and starting position was critical for me to be able to follow him during his steep but slow dive to the runway. I had to be a couple hundred feet at his four o'clock dirtied up with the landing gear, flaps, and speed brakes extended when he deployed the spin recovery chute and pushed over into his dive. I momentarily delayed lowering the nose to stay slightly above him, as I started following him in his steep dive. Eventually, I wouldn't be able to stay with him, slowly gaining speed and pulling ahead of him even as I slowly decreased the dive angle trying to prevent my speed from getting too much faster. Some times my timing maneuver would be exact and we'd be leveling off a couple of thousand of feet above landing pattern altitude observing Jerry touch down on the runway. Other times, we'd be off a little and we'd be level looking back at Jerry still descending towards the runway. Luckily, I was always in position for what the photographer needed to document, the deep stalls and the spin recovery chute deployment. Once the chute was deployed and Jerry started his dive towards the runway, the photographer's job was completed.

By the fall of 1969, I had started my last course of my Master's degree program and knew I'd be graduating in January 1970. I submitted a volunteer statement for assignment to Southeast Asia upon completion of the program. I wanted to make sure I went back in fighters so I listed my six preferences in priority order. My first choice was A-7's because it was the newest weapon system. Second, I listed F-4's with a consecutive follow-on tour to USAFE. Third was the Thud, the assignment I thought most likely I would get since it was my high time and most recent fighter. I followed this with the Hun, then the A-1 and finally the AO-37.

I was surprised when I received orders to the 35th Tactical Fighter Wing Safety Office flying F-100s at Phan Rang AB, Republic of Vietnam. I wasn't too sure the assignment as a Wing Safety Officer was a career enhancement assignment but at least I was getting back into fighters.

Since it was a Permanent Change of Station (PCS), we had to vacate our base housing. The base allowed families to remain in the base trailer park so as we jokingly said in our family, my wife became "Queen of the doublewides". This option provided the least disruptive move, same friends, school, and still within two hours of family. I left for Luke AFB, AZ, in early February, 1970 to get recurrent in the F-100. It had been six and a half years since I had last flown her!

Chapter 6: Hun Combat

The F-100 recurrency course at Luke was short and fast, flying only 17 sorties for 23.5 hours in less than a month. I immediately felt right at home, the unique engine fumes in the cockpit was like a shot of smelling salts arousing all my sensory perceptions of the Hun, even after an absence of six and a half years. It felt so good to get back in a fighter cockpit; all the natural reflexes peculiar to flying the Hun came back quickly. During my third flight, the first solo in a "D", the left wing dropped just as we broke ground while I was on the wing of a formation take-off. I surprised myself when I instinctively used right rudder to pick the wing up!

The course was cut short when the last two phases, air refueling and night weapons delivery were waved. F-100 operations in South Vietnam did not require air-refueling support; when tankers were not available for the air-refueling phase, it was easy for higher headquarters to wave this training. Waving night weapons delivery on the other hand was not as logical. Night missions were being conducted by Huns in South Vietnam so this was training that should have been accomplished. As unbelievable as it was, there were no flares available to conduct the training. The phase was waved on the grounds that our graduation could not be delayed waiting for flares to become available.

There were only four of us in the class, all destined for the 35th TFW at Phan Rang. I knew George Weeks from a previous assignment in Japan six years earlier. Bob Hoover was a test pilot I knew from Edwards AFB. We finished our recurrency training the third week in March, giving me about twenty days before having to leave for Vietnam.

When that day came, it was one of the hardest departures of my career. The family had gone through a lot of separations when I was assigned to F-105's in Japan, none of them as difficult as this one. These last 33 months at Edwards had been wonderful for the family; I guess I didn't realize how much we all had become accustomed to me being home. The drive from Edwards to Fox Field in Lancaster took about 40 minutes on a long straight road. We were all pretty quiet in the car as I drove to the airport to be dropped off. I didn't realize how difficult it had been for Pat. I didn't find out until I returned from Vietnam that she had tears running down her cheeks most of the drive back to Edwards. The Beatles' "Hey

(USAF Photo)
**F-100 1970 Recurrency Class, Luke AFB, Arizona.
Left to Right: Maj. Weeks, Maj. Graf, Author, and Maj. Hoover**

Jude" was playing on the radio and to this day, whenever I hear it, it reminds me of that long drive, it was a very sad day.

It didn't get any easier. My parents met me at the Los Angeles airport during my layover waiting for my chartered flight. This was the first time I was saying good-by to them as I was leaving for combat. When it came time for me to board, my Dad who was getting along in age, hugged me and said he hoped he would still be around when I returned. I didn't think of my Dad as being that old and it surprised me he said that. I responded positively with, "Of course you will". As I finished hugging my mother, she touched my face and just gave me a smile; I don't think she could say anything. I kissed her on the check, turned and walked down the passageway to board the plane wondering if I had done the right thing to volunteer to go back.

First stop on the way to Nam was Clark AB, The Philippines, for Jungle Survival Training better known as "Snake School". In the classroom phase, we were taught what was edible in the jungle, the various poisonous plants, snakes and animals that might be encountered, and techniques for surviving in the jungle.

The classroom phase was followed with a field exercise out in the jungle where we had to evade being caught by the negrito (indigenous natives to the area) populace who were rewarded with a small sack of rice for each "capture" made. My partner and I survived not being captured which was very unusual. It wasn't that we were that good at evading but more likely because we might have pressed the gaming area borders when we traveled about a third of the way down into an off limits deep canyon. "If you ain't cheating, you ain't trying!"

Reporting to Phan Rang, I was assigned to the 35th TFW in the Wing Safety Office, attached to the 352nd TFS for flying. In the 352nd, I was

(Stock Photo)

Phan Rang AB, South Vietnam.

shocked to find out my 470 hours of 100 time made me the third high time F-100 pilot in the squadron! Eight years earlier, when I reported to my first operational F-100 squadron, most of the older pilots had a couple thousand hours of F-100 experience; the F-100 fleet experience had certainly been diluted. The fact I was relatively high experienced may have been my saving grace; usually Wing Wienies were not highly thought of. I was assigned a bedroom in the 352nd building, which also helped establish camaraderie with the squadron members. Each squadron building had a small lounge in the center with bedrooms down hallways that branched out either side of the central lounge. We had a small bar in

(Personal Photo)
352nd TFS Lounge with "Blue Velvet" Hanging on Wall.

the lounge where most of the guys hung out socializing after the day's flying. The bartender was a shapely attractive young Vietnamese lady who poured the drinks from behind the bar. The squadron commander took me aside one evening and chastised me, accusing me of ogling her bodacious tatas (I thought that's what fighter pilots did!). I got the feeling he didn't like me. He let me know that she was the flight surgeon's girlfriend and that she was off limits. I wasn't happy with his little lecture and I was insulted by his insinuation I was interested in doing more than just admire a shapely young lady! I was glad he wasn't representative of how the rest of the squadron felt towards me but this was not a good relationship with a commanding officer. I got along fine with the other guys and developed some special friendships in the unit.

The squadron had a mascot named "Beaver". Fighter pilots haven't changed through the ages and always seemed to have the same thing on their minds. Twenty-six years earlier, my brother's squadron, the 345th Fighter Sqdn, in World War II had a mascot named "Snatch".

(Personal Photo)
Author's Squadron Mascot Named "Beaver".

(Personal Photo)
Author's Brother, Gil, P-39 & P-47 WW II Fighter Pilot With Squadron Mascot "Snatch"

Soon after getting settled in the squadron, I received a letter from a friend at Edwards informing me that Jerry Gentry had ejected from the F-4 modified for the spin test project when it got into a spin and the spin recovery chute separated from the plane upon deployment. What an unfortunate accident and fickled fate, the spin chute was successfully deployed at the end of each flight and the one time it really was needed, it failed!

Combat in South Vietnam seemed so benign compared to what I had experienced flying Thuds over the North, yet, we still suffered losses. A young Lieutenant had just returned from a few days' visit to a small Army outpost to experience a ground pounder's life. He told the grunts he would come by and put on a little air show for them on his next flight. On his first low-level pass over the outpost, he pulled up, did a barrel roll, and hit the ground at the bottom of the maneuver, killing himself. The accident was complicated by the fact that the wingman on the flight was my future boss in the Wing Safety office who was new and had just recently arrived. They tried to pin supervisory error on him since he was the ranking man on the flight. But he was too new, not in command of the flight, and didn't know the Lieutenant was going to do the barrel roll. There was no way he could be held responsible, the Lieutenant had briefed they would only do a low level pass; but still, not a great way to start out in a new assignment.

My first sortie was a local area check out in the front seat of an "F" with "Chestnut", a high time crusty senior Major in the rear cockpit. Two days later, I flew my second combat mission, this time as number two in a "D". Our missions were either preplanned hitting lines of communications, small bridges, or structures in areas controlled by the Viet Cong, or scrambled off alert to provide Close Air Support under the control of a Forward Air Controller (FAC) for troops in contact with enemy forces.

Because of my relative high F-100 time compared to others in the squadron, I was quickly upgraded to flight lead status. My check ride consisted of me leading the check pilot, "Chestnut" again, on a preplanned two-ship flight. The mission called for us to rendezvous with an O-1 Birddog FAC and strike whatever target he designated. When we reached the rendezvous point, the area was covered with a low broken cloud deck. I made contact with our FAC on mission frequency and spotted two O-1s in the general area so I asked the FAC to rock his wings for positive identification. He acknowledged, "Rocking my wings." I immediately picked him out of the two O-1s. "Tally Ho" I said letting him know I had him in sight. He acknowledged, "The target is up ahead, follow me". He continued his mission brief, giving us a description of the target, direction he wanted us to attack from, location and altitude he would be holding, etc., all while heading towards the target. We were high at his seven o'clock following him. When he disappeared under a good size cloud, it presented a good time for me to take my eyes off him and do a quick check of the cockpit, fuel check, weapons arming etc. After he came out from under the cloud he said, "target dead ahead, rolling in to mark". I waited to see his smoke. Next transmission was "Okay, hit a 100 feet past my smoke, I'm breaking right for holding". The O-1 I was watching hadn't done a thing, it was still pressing on straight and level! I said "Rock your wings, I might have lost you when you went under that last big cloud". He acknowledged and the O-1 I had my eyes on wasn't rocking his wings. Evidently, when he had flown under that last huge cloud, he must have crossed paths with another O-1 and I picked up the wrong one as they came out from underneath the cloud. What an embarrassing screw up, especially during a Flight Lead check ride. After a few more radio calls, we reformed on the correct O-1 and executed the mission. Luckily, we hit his target and he was pleased with the results and gave us a good Battle Damage Assessment (BDA) report.

"Chestnut", usually a very serious guy, chuckled as he debriefed the rendezvous portion of the check ride. He thought I recovered well re-converging with the correct FAC, attacking the target and leading him. I came out of the debriefing room a Flight Lead.

After being in country a month, I had flown 28 combat missions and accrued 40 hours of Hun time. Also, in that period, I'd flown four Night Owl missions, a totally new experience. Three of the Night Owl missions were on consecutive nights. This was only the beginning. My reputation from Edwards of never saying no, or enough is enough followed me because the squadron dumped the night missions on me. I ended flying 17 more Night Owl missions for a total of 21 sorties dive bombing at night under flares. The Wing Commander had taken note of how much night flying I had been doing. At my going away party he got pretty good laughs when in his speech, he mentioned every time he called the squadron in the evening to speak with me, he'd be told I was night flying. He followed that with, "That was pretty drastic measures to take to avoid having to speak with me!"

Although I didn't have data to substantiate it, it felt like the squadron also scheduled me a disproportionate amount of times in the "F"; why not, give it to the Wing Wienie and save the "D" slots for the "regular" squadron pilots! But actually, it really wasn't that bad since I had been upgraded to an IP which always made me the pilot in command in an "F". I was surprised that the IP upgrade program consisted of only a single check flight. My check ride was scheduled with Doug Lea, a pilot who would become a great friend in later years when we served together in an F-5 Tac Fighter Training Squadron. Doug briefed that he needed to see me do three landings from the back seat when we returned from our mission. Other than the fact that I had never done a back seat landing in the Super Sabre, what would be the big deal? Except for the weapons delivery, I flew the entire mission from the rear cockpit, including making the take-off.

Then the moment of truth! It was time to do what I had never done before in a Hun. Ask a fighter pilot to do a roll, invariably, he'll do it to the left. That is because it is easier to push the control stick to the left than pull to the right. I was pleased we were landing runway 22, which was a left hand pattern, the preferred left! But alas, it was no help at all. To describe the resultant landing as a controlled crash would be a stretch. Only a Navy carrier pilot would consider it a normal landing! As we hit the runway and I poured the coals to go around, from the front seat I heard, "Jesus Christ! You pass, I don't want to have to go through another one of those again!" Needless to say, Doug took control of the airplane and made the next landing a full stop. That landing from the back seat was the worst landing of my entire career -- and I passed.

A friendly Lt. Col. usually filled the rear pit in most of my "F" flights. I thought it strange that he never had any interest in getting some stick time whenever I offered him control of the aircraft. Then I found out he was the Wing navigation officer, another Wing Wienie just like me. He appeared to enjoy flying, never turning down flight opportunities.

About half way through my tour I took leave and visited Ray Curtis, a very dear friend from Edwards, now stationed in Saigon. I had no problem getting a space available flight to Tan Son Nhut AB near Saigon. Spent the weekend with him and he showed me around but we didn't wonder too far out from his hotel which had been turned into a headquarters. We visited the tennis courts on the hotel's grounds and watched players properly clad in white tennis sports attire playing.

Everything was so proper and colonial; it was hard to think we were in a war zone.

On my return trip I got stuck at the Tan Son Nhut terminal trying to get space available back to Phan Rang. There just weren't any flights headed there, or at least that is what the personnel behind the space "A" counter were telling me. I was getting concerned, then I heard a voice, "Vic, What are you doing here?" I turned to see who it was and to my pleasant surprise, it was my Lt. Col navigator who frequently flew in the back seat of my "F". I told him I had been visiting a close friend in Saigon but was now stuck trying to get back to Phan Rang. The Lt. Col said, "Wait here, let me see what I can do" and left headed out towards the ramp. After a while, he returned and said he had checked with the pilot of the C-123 he was riding and that he had gotten clearance from the pilot to have me join them. They had two stops at remote bases to drop off fuel before heading to their final destination, Phan Rang. That Colonel sure loved to fly, and he sure was a lifesaver.

When I boarded the C-123, the loadmaster showed me to a web seat clear of a huge fuel bladder strapped to the floor taking up most of the cargo bay, the Lt. Col went up into the crew compartment with the pilot and the co-pilot and we flew to the first of the two scheduled remote fields.

I couldn't see much out of the small porthole window behind me or across from me but from the engine sounds I could sense we were in a steep descent for landing. The touchdown was more of a controlled crash with the immediate roaring sound of the engine props reversing, rapid deceleration throwing me sideways against the cockpit bulkhead, and a lot of brown dust blowing past the small porthole windows. When we climbed out of the "Provider" I was startled by the small size of the dirt runway we had just landed on, carved out of the jungle. Calling this a remote base was a huge overstatement. I noticed I was the only person standing there without a side arm. Even the C-123 crew, including my Lt. Col was armed. The 123 loadmaster was busy hooking up a fuel hose to the fuel bladder while two bare-chested young troops were dragging the other end of the hose towards several large barrels between two Cobra gunships parked at the edge of the jungle. The Lt. Col informed me the two guys dragging the other end of the hose were crewmembers of one of the Cobra gunships. I couldn't believe it, how could that be, they looked like young teenage boys in high school. I watched in amazement as everyone went about transferring fuel from the bladder while the 123 pilot and co-pilot did their aircraft pre-flight. It was

Delivering Avgas to Remote Army Base.
(Personal Photo)

obvious this was going to be a minimum time turn around. The Lt. Col continued briefing me on the base and its operations. It was loud and clear this place wasn't the most secure and safest place to be.

Looking around, seeing these young troops not much older than twenty years and responsible for these gunships, the pilot skills of getting a C-123 into a little patch of dirt classified as a runway, gave me a new appreciation for the non-fighter pilot warrior. It exposed me to a new and very different view of the war.

Fighter pilots are egotistical because they are usually at the top of their graduating pilot training class and know they have to be good to get a fighter assignment. My C-123 experience made me think possibly the only difference between pilots is the fighter pilot has a natural aptitude for flying, while all others grow into it; with a few exceptions, we were all generally equal. The abilities of that C-123 pilot more than impressed me, it humbled me.

The Wing always had two birds on alert in the closest aircraft shelter by the end of the runway. One Hun would be loaded with four cans of napalm while the other would have four Mk-82 500 pound bombs, usually with Snake Eye fins (high drag retardation fins for low altitude delivery).

One of my most anxious moments of my tour was a scramble where my wingman and I were vectored to a FAC requesting air support for troops in contact. In bound to the target, we made contact with the FAC who proceeded to brief us on the situation. The friendlies were on one side of a small river in a firefight with a larger Viet Cong force on the other side. When we reached their location, the jungle was so thick we could not see the river under the canopy foliage and were having difficulty identifying their exact location; it all looked the same. The FAC informed us the friendlies were going to mark their spot with white smoke and the target would be a hundred yards to the north of the smoke. A few moments later purple smoke started seeping out between the jungle trees and the FAC got all excited yelling into his radio, "Hit that smoke, that's the bad guys, they are trying to spoof us!"

His call concerned me. Our guys were going to mark their spot with smoke, now because it wasn't the color expected; I was supposed to bomb the smoke? What if there was a miscommunication about the color? Concerned about friendly fire, I questioned the FAC's instructions and requested verification these weren't the friendlies. He was adamant in his response, again saying "Hit the smoke!' I did as instructed, and pickled my bombs off, thinking this guy better be right or I won't be able to live with myself if I was responsible for a friendly fire incident. Such is the fog and stress of war!

There was an Aussie detachment of Canberra bombers at Phan Rang. One day there was a notice on our squadron flight scheduling board asking if anyone was interested in getting a flight with the Aussies. Always looking for adventure, I said I'd go. The Canberra is a two-man crew bomber with pilot and a bombardier/navigator. For my orientation flight, I was given the bomb/nav's seat behind the bulkhead separating the pilot and the bomb/nav. British and Aussie Canberras do not have the canopy enclosing the pilot and backseater together like in the US B-57 version of the Canberra; all I had for looking outside was a very small rectangular side window. The Aussie bomb/nav took a jump seat in the small passageway next to the pilot for the take-off. After climb out and level off, the bomb/nav took his parachute off so he could squeeze into the bombardier's position in the nose. What a concept, who would design a battle station so small the combatant could not wear a parachute during the critical time of being over a target? Must not have been a combatant.

(Personal Photo)

Author Gets a Combat Mission in an Aussie Canberra at Phan Rang.

Before squeezing into the nose, he turned to me and patted the jump seat and motioned for me to take his place, saying it was a better view from there. I had to agree; it was just slightly better than having to stare straight onto a bulkhead. But the seat was still so low you could not see out over the instrument panel; you were eye level with the pilot's butt right next to you. For the remainder of the flight, all I could see was blue sky if I looked almost straight up, and the pilot constantly moving the flight control yoke keeping our aircraft in formation with the other Canberra in the flight. We delivered our bombs straight and level and returned for a TACAN approach to Phan Rang. Before reaching the TACAN initial fix, I moved back to my original position so the bomb/nav could have the jump seat.

I found the experience flying with the Aussies interesting and a square filler, I could now claim to have flown in a Canberra, not to be confused with a B-57!

Right after my Aussie flight, I was also offered a chance to do an F-100 Functional Check Flight (FCF). Major Graf, one of the pilots with whom I went through Luke when I re-qualified in the F-100 was assigned as the Wing Maintenance Officer and all he flew were FCF's. He had three FCF's due and wanted me to take one. I told him I'd need to review the Dash-6 FCF Pilot's Hand Book and learn the FCF profile, but sure, I'd do it. He told me it wouldn't be necessary to do a complete FCF profile. The airplane was consistently being written up for excessive fumes in the cockpit. Graf just wanted me to take it up on a local flight and check if the fumes really were too strong. This was an inherent characteristic of the F-100. I figured they would have to be really bad to be written up. I asked what about FCF Orders, I'd have to be on them to be legal. He said he'd take care of it.

I checked the aircraft forms to see what maintenance actions had been taken to correct the write up. I was surprised to see this was going to be the third FCF for the same problem. The first corrective action was to retighten some lines. That didn't correct the problem. Now maintenance had replaced some parts and tightened more lines.

I started up, did the standard ground checks, and taxied out for take-off; yes the plane had the unique fume smell of an F-100. On the runway, I slowly advanced the throttle to 100% and the fumes got stronger. The thought of aborting raced through my mind but I quickly discarded it figuring if it got any worse, I'd fly around sucking up 100% oxygen. I flew a local flight around the area for a while on 100% oxygen and then went to normal to check the fumes; I thought they were slightly stronger than normal but bearable. Before returning to land I rolled inverted and shook the plane slightly to check for any loose items; the only thing I got was minimal dirt and dust. When I returned to the ramp, I signed off the discrepancy write up to the relief of maintenance. The flight was a nice change from the daily combat routine.

With deference to the F-4's doing dangerous but effective Night Owl work on the Mu Gia Pass Trail, other than slinging yourself at the ground at night, Night Owl missions in our area were fairly mundane; but the potential for anxious or exciting moments was always there. During one of my later Night Owl missions, I was scheduled with a new Lieutenant as my number 2. This being his first Night Owl mission, I made sure I covered all items on the briefing guide, especially those items particular to the Night Owl mission.

As briefed, I set up a rectangular pattern offset up wind from the target. We were self-illuminating, releasing our own parachute floating MK 24 Mod O flares on the downwind leg with a turn to a base leg from which we would roll in for our dive bomb pass at the target. After making my two runs at the target, it was my wingman's turn. My flares had already extinguished and the area had returned to total darkness. Only a few visible stars, the navigation lights of my wingman across the pattern from me, and something burning on the ground where I had dropped my bombs, distinguished what was sky and what was ground. My wingman was on the downwind leg ready to start illuminating in preparation for his attack. Suddenly, he yelled, "My flare pod is on fire!" I responded, "JETTISON IT!" Following his shadowy silhouette of his navigation lights, I saw a tumbling fireball streak away towards the ground. My next transmission was "Are you okay?" In a much calmer voice he responded, "I think so."

Evidently, the flares ignited when he pickled but got stuck and were burning in the pod. It was a terrifying first Night Owl experience for the young Lieutenant, one I'm sure he would never forget.

Phan Rang is located in the southern portion of II Corps, close to 400 miles from the DMZ. Most of our missions were in II and III Corps. I was surprised one day when we were tasked to do a road cut very near the DMZ in I Corps; making it the longest mission of my South Vietnam tour. I wondered why we'd be flying that distance when Da Nang AB, another F-100 base, was so much closer. As Alfred Lord Tennyson penned, "Ours is not to reason why, but just do and die!"

I led the mission with an experienced wingman as 2. The target area was perfectly clear without a cloud in sight. We met up with our FAC in an O-1 Birddog who briefed the target, a road winding north in very mountainous terrain near the DMZ. He rolled in and marked the spot he wanted us to bomb to form a road cut. I rolled in, pickled off my four Mk-82 500 pound slick bombs (None retarded fins) and pulled off to the west as he had briefed. Before I could look back to check my results, I heard the excited FAC call out, "That's a shack, Lead!" (A bullseye). I spotted where my bombs had hit and saw number 2 in his dive just as he released his bombs. Continuing a circular climb back to where I had rolled in, I saw 2's bombs hit the center of the road about fifty feet next to mine. The FAC went crazy! He asked what unit we were from and what dive angle were we using. I told him we were doing 30-degree dive. He replied we were "gutsy" but "good", giving me the impression

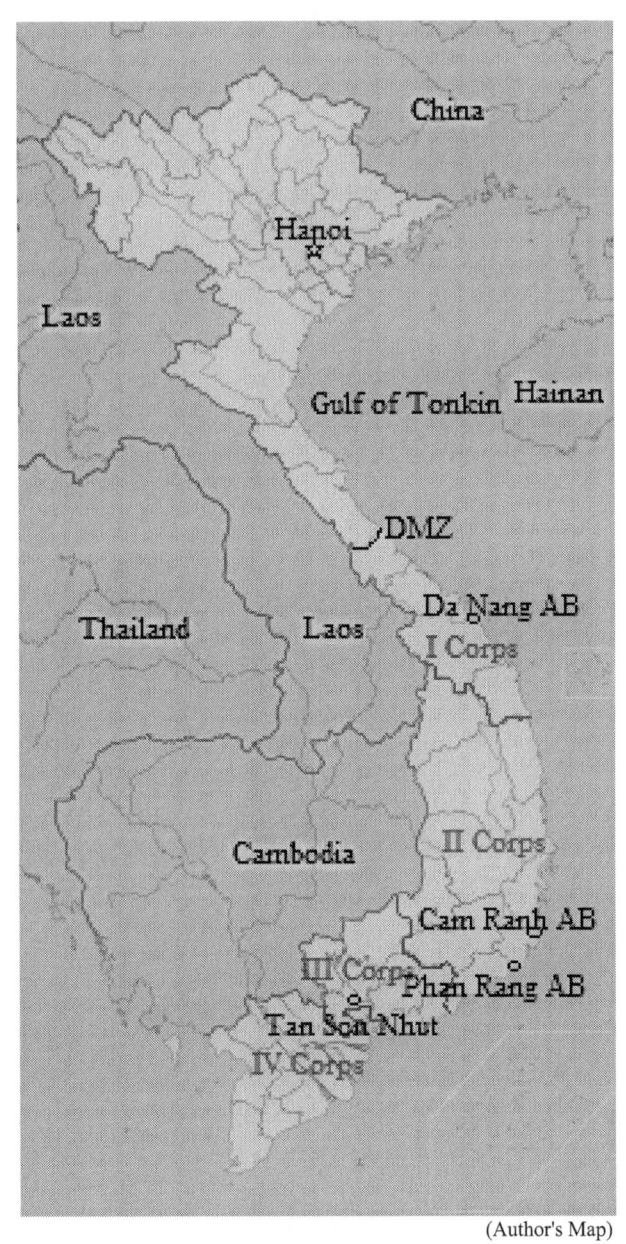

(Author's Map)
Most Phan Rang AB Missions Were in II & III Corps. Author's Furthest Mission Was at the Laotian Vietnamese Border by the DMZ.

he thought the threat warranted using a 45-degree dive. This was a piece of cake compared to bombing missions over North Vietnam! He credited us with 100% target destroyed in his BDA report.

My wingman and I felt pretty good about our bombing that day. The gun camera processing shop the next day contacted us, saying we should come down and check our film from the previous day. I never checked my gun camera film; I couldn't imagine anything worthwhile ever showing up on it. But we complied with their suggestion and reviewed the gun camera film. We were surprised to see a couple streaks of 37mm AAA come across our nose during the dive bomb run. Had no idea we were being shot at on that mission. Guess that is why the FAC insinuated that a higher dive angle would have been more judicious.

Not all missions were as effective as the road cut near the DMZ. As luck would have it, I was on the Squadron Commander's wing as number 2 attacking a wooden bridge over a deep gully when I missed big time, twice! We were under control of a talkative FAC who was not pleased with our performance; we were having a bad day. We were doing low angle 15 degree dive with MK-82 Snake Eyes. Lead missed just short of the bridge but close enough to cause some damage. The FAC acting like a cheerleader, was encouraging me with a pep talk after Lead's near miss. "Okay 2, you can do better than that, finish off the bridge on your pass!" Unfortunately, my bombs went just over the bridge resulting in a long hit by a larger margin than Lead's short hit.

Lead's second pass was almost identical to his first; the bridge was still standing after his pass. The FAC was becoming agitated. "Oh come on guys, you can do better than that! Two, come on, finish it off, you're cleared in." It just wasn't our day; we looked like amateurs. My second attempt was worse than my first try. Other than "Oh my God", the FAC was speechless. He finally asked, "Ready for BDA?" After Lead said he was ready, the FAC, in a disgusting voice said, "I'll give you 5% target destroyed.

The squadrons threw hard drinking going away parties. Dangerously, those in command from the Wing Commander down, were willing to look the other way and ignore Air Force regulations regarding drinking within 24 hours of flying. Too many pilots were flying within the 24-hour restriction. I was one of them one time, but it only took one flight hung over to realize how stupid and dangerous that was. I and a young Lieutenant I was mentoring had partied hard the night before his practice flight to upgrade to flight lead status. We were both hung over when we reported for the first flight of the day very early the next morning. The Lieutenant had to excuse himself several times to go worship at the porcelain altar while trying to brief the mission. I thought, hmm, this is not good. Shortly after returning to continue the briefing I had to do the same thing. After up chucking a couple of times, you get the false sensation that you are feeling better. All we need is a little shot of 100% oxygen once we get out to the airplane -- wrong! Taxiing onto the runway, I notice Lead had failed to set his flaps for take-off. I radioed, "Lead, check flaps" and then rechecked mine and found I hadn't set mine either. By now, I had gotten all the clues that we were in no shape to be in an airplane but I stupidly ignored them.

On the way to the target, I was breathing in as much 100% oxygen which helped me feel a little better; I'm sure Lead was doing the same or at least I hoped he was.

Lead rolled in for a 15-degree dive bomb pass, releasing one bomb. He had briefed we'd drop singly to get as much practice doing low angle dive. When I did my 4 "G" pull out from my dive, I almost passed out. My "G" tolerance had been greatly diminished by the alcohol. I had noticed that even at two "Gs", I was starting to black out. The light finally came on and I called Lead to get rid of all his bombs on the next pass and to watch his "Gs". He acknowledged, we terminated bombing with the second pass, and returned to base. That was a hard lesson learned and we were both fortunate we hadn't blacked out and flown into the ground!

Nearing the end of my tour, there was a mass briefing of all the pilots in the base theater. Security line badges were checked at entry, generating curiosity of what was this all about. The Wing Commander began the meeting by emphasizing the sensitive nature of what was to follow and instructing us that we could not discuss it with anyone outside the theater. He then turned the meeting over to the Deputy Commander for Operations who broke the news that starting the next day, our combat operations would be extended into Cambodia!

This was totally unexpected. Whatever your opinion of President Nixon, you had to give the Commander-in-Chief credit for having big "gonads". He was determined to end US involvement in Southeast Asia, honorably, and was pulling out all the stops in the conduct of the war to achieve this goal. Cambodia had been a long time sanctuary for Communist forces in South Vietnam. They would cross into Cambodia to lick their wounds and regroup anytime they took a beating from the

ARVN without the fear of being pursued. Now the ARVN was going to be allowed to follow the enemy into Cambodia and we were going to provide them air support.

Cambodian missions brought about two changes. First, for the first time in my Phan Rang tour, we got air refueling tanker support; secondly, we started flying in four ship flights. This presented a challenge, many of our pilots had never air refueled, that training having been waived in their check out similar to my class. For myself, it had been over seven years since I had poked an F-100 probe into a basket and it had been against a KB-50, never a KC-135.

In one of the first Cambodian missions, I was scheduled to lead a four ship in which only number 4 and I had air refueling F-100 experience. Aware of this, I spent extra time instructing the two inexperienced flight members on aerial refueling techniques during the flight briefing.

When we hit the KC-135, I was first to try hooking up and surprisingly; I had no problems at all. I'm sure my many hook ups with the KC-135 drogue configuration during my F-105 tours in Southeast Asia contributed to making it look easy. My inexperienced flight members flying off to the side waiting their turn had an opportunity to observe the technique I had briefed. I hoped the saying "a picture is worth a thousand words" would prove true when it was their turn.

Number 2 in the flight, was a low time F-100 Lt. Col whose total high time in other aircraft showed as he successfully hooked up after a couple of stabs at the basket.

Then it was my Lieutenant buddy's turn I was mentoring. He had the most difficulty hooking up. He was stabilizing too far back from the basket and chasing it as he moved forward. He came close a couple of times, hitting the rim of the basket with the probe. I didn't like giving a lot of verbal in flight instruction. I thought it was a stronger learning experience for the student to analyze what he was doing wrong and correct it if he could. But it was getting time to help and I planned to tell him to stabilize closer to the basket if he missed on his next try. As it was, I didn't have to say anything as he finally succeeded hooking up; but it wasn't pretty.

Tim followed the Lieutenant and his experienced showed as he hooked up on his first attempt.

After the flight, as I completed the mission debrief, Tim asked me to stay, he wanted to discuss the mission privately with me. When we were left alone, Tim started in on me, saying I needed to take more command of the flight. He thought I had let number 3 go too far trying to figure out how to hook up. I appreciated him giving me his opinion in private and even though he was closer to correct than wrong, I thought he was a little more critical and upset with the way I lead the flight than he needed to be. To each his own!

Providing close air support in Cambodia was easier than in South Vietnam, at least in the areas of Cambodia I flew. The vegetation in Cambodia was not nearly as thick as in Vietnam, making it easier to locate and identify enemy ground troops. It wasn't only easier locating positions, but for the first time, I actually saw the enemy crouching in a ditch along a tree line I was strafing. My first vision of humans in my gun sight suddenly brought the brutality of war to the forefront. My combat experience of bombing, or rocketing roads, bridges, and structures was much easier; it was always killing inanimate objects. White smoke from a machinegun shooting back from the ditch just as suddenly made me realize they were trying to kill me as well. War is an ugly thing!

I don't know how many missions I flew in Cambodia; unfortunately, the mission code in my Air Force flight records did not differentiate missions by country, but I estimate it was a hand full.

With the Cambodian campaign, I had flown combat in all four corners of the Southeast Asian War; Laos, North Vietnam, South Vietnam, and Cambodia.

Chapter 7: Academy Award Performance

    I didn't feel like an actual flying safety officer. I had not been through the formal USAF safety officer course at Norton AFB, California and was really learning through on-the-job training with this assignment. I was pretty sure I received this position because some detailer in officer's assignments mistook my recent graduation from my USC Master's course for the safety course originally taught by USC at Norton. The USC Master's Aerospace Operations Management degree I had just completed, was titled "Operations and Safety Management" when I first started the program.
    Historically, the flying safety field is not a career advancing position because it is as close to a no win situation as you can get but with luck, survive. If you have the misfortune of having an ineffective safety program, you get a lot of unfavorable exposure and interaction with the Wing hierarchy and become a standout among bad press. On the other hand, if you have an outstanding effective program, and there are no incidents/accidents, there is very little interaction with the hierarchy; you get no press and become just one among many officers in the Wing.
    I felt like I was falling into the first category of too much interaction with the Wing higher ups for the wrong reasons. The Wing was experiencing about one tree strike a month, luckily without loss of life or aircraft. But it was only a matter of when, not if. Our missions mostly involved low altitude weapons delivery that left little room for error. Finally, the Wing Commander had had enough and directed me to schedule a meeting of all pilots to address the problem. I didn't know what I could tell the group that would be new or they already didn't know. My boss suggested using my artistic talents and draw diagrams, using the old adage, a picture is worth a thousand words. I followed his advice but they were really ineffective for such a large crowd with only those near the front being able to make them out. Nonetheless, we had the meeting and the Wing Commander ended up being the more effective speaker. When he spoke, he was blunt, to the point, and threatening. He said one tree strike a month was one too many. This had to stop before someone gets killed. He did not want to have to write a letter home to a loved one saying "I regret to inform you your son or husband killed himself attacking a Viet Cong tree!' Next person to get a

tree strike, you might as well head east out over the water until you run out of fuel, eject and keep swimming because your career will be over. With that, he walked off the stage. The mass of pilots stood there in silence!

About a week after the meeting, I was leading George in a two ship bombing mission. I had known George from before, we were in the same F-100 recurrency class at Luke just prior to coming to Phan Rang and in Japan years earlier when we were in the same Wing flying F-105s.

(Personal Photo)

Literally a "Tree Busting" Mission.
Hun With Mk-82 Bombs With Fuse Extenders.

As I came off my bomb pass, I looked back to check my hits and watch George make his delivery. As he came off the target, I saw a little cloud of vapor momentarily form between his plane and the jungle foliage. I also thought I saw what looked like metal parts separating from his aircraft. It happened so quickly, I wasn't sure what I had observed, whatever it was, it just didn't look normal. My attention then momentarily diverted to his exploding ordnance. When I refocused my attention to George, his flying appeared a little erratic so I asked him if he was okay. He came back with some garbled response I couldn't understand. I said, "Say again" as I cautiously attempted to rejoin the erratically flying F-100. His reply was some other nonsensible message.

I joined up a couple hundred feet off his wing; there was damage underneath the fuselage from the trailing edge of the wing all the way back to the tail with small pieces of tree wedged in panel crevices. He continued to fly unsteadily unable to maintain straight and level. I finally said, "Two, go 100% oxygen." No acknowledgement but I could see him looking around the cockpit like he was confused and searching for the location of the oxygen panel. He eventually looked over in the direction of the lower right in the cockpit and reached over as if he was selecting 100% oxygen. He then looked over in my direction in an unexpressive stare. I started giving him directions, telling him he had the lead and gave him a heading and altitude to fly. After a short hesitation, he responded and started following my directions. As the flight progressed towards home plate, his flying became more steady and responsive, even giving me a head nod with a thumbs up.

Nearing Phan Rang, I contacted the tower and told them we were inbound declaring an emergency of a possible hypoxic pilot in a damaged plane and requesting a straight-in approach with impoundment of the aircraft upon arrival.

I informed George I would chase him down to landing and then I'd go around. He acknowledged with a head nod. By the time we started letting down, he was flying normal and I was feeling better about his ability to make a safe landing.

On the ground, George was already out of the aircraft by the time I landed and met up with him. There was a crowd of maintenance and ops people already around him and his plane that had been impounded. First thing I looked for was to see if the Wing Commander was among them; he wasn't, good, so far! Reverting to my Wing safety instincts, I told maintenance I thought there might have been oxygen problems of one form or another, including contaminants. I wrote up the discrepancy in the aircraft forms for George who was still "acting" slightly abnormal. Talking with the squadron Maintenance Officer, I told him they needed to have the aircraft oxygen tank checked at a lab for contaminants after they had finished with all their other checks; he agreed.

Meanwhile the DCO came up and began questioning me on what had happened. As I told the story and my suspicion that George's judgment might have been impaired because of insufficient oxygen he started to look at me with a jaundice eye -- really? I had a difficult time keeping a straight face but managed to remain serious, saying we'll never really know until we get the findings of the investigation.

The DCO ordered that George be taken to the hospital and tested for toxins; something that I thought had the potential of weakening any credibility for hypoxia being the cause of the tree strike and needed to be avoided. This could be the "fly in the ointment". I never knew if a hospital evaluation was ever done and results ever produced.

Maintenance found no discrepancies in their inspection of the oxygen fittings and the oxygen regulator. The oxygen tank had to be shipped to a lab in the Philippines and we were still waiting for results weeks later.

Meanwhile, all this emphasis on possible physiological problems was keeping the focus off of the real problem... another tree busting episode! How long could this last? I'm sure George hoped it lasted until the next incident pushed his into the abyss of history. With no direct findings obtained on the hypoxic theory, the tree strike slowly faded away and George escaped what could have been a career ending event. I didn't believe this was by accident, George was a good officer and pilot and my sense was someone with clout was allowing this incident to disappear with time. He survived the tree strike and completed his tour. He deserved it! It was an Academy Award performance.

Some incidents were not self-induced as in the case of tree strikes. I observed a landing F-100 lose all its utility hydraulic pressure right after

(USAF Photo)

Hun Ran Into Aircraft Shelter After Loss of Nose Wheel Steering and Wheel Brakes Due to Total Utility Hydraulics Failure.

it turned off the runway. The pilot realizing he had no steering or stopping capability, desperately tried to get peoples' attention, dropping his tail hook which was the Wing signal for an aircraft on the ground needing help. He was frantically waving his arms out of the cockpit and giving the "chock me" hand signal whenever he could get someone's attention, but no one ever reacted! In desperation to slow down, he stopcocked the throttle shutting down the engine.

I was witnessing this from the alert pad, too far away to be able to get someone's attention to help before he slowly disappeared behind the alert pad. The Hun finally stopped when it ran into the edge of an aircraft shelter, fortunately without any injury to personnel other than to the F-100!

In an opportunity to get away from being in the line of fire every time there was an incident, I accepted the squadron's request to put me on the schedule to deliver an F-100 to the major overhaul facility in Taipei, Taiwan. I was familiar with the depot facility at Taipei having delivered and picked up F-105s while I was stationed in Japan four years earlier. Since I was the experienced pilot in the flight, I was scheduled as the flight lead with a young lieutenant on my wing delivering a second F-100. Da Nang had an F-4 for delivery to the facility and we were

(Personal Photo)
My Wingman on Ferry Flight to Depot at Taipei, Taiwan

(Personal Photo)
Wingman Nice And Close During Ferry Flight.

to rendezvous with it at a specified point and time off the coast of Da Nang.

Approaching the rendezvous area, we made radio contact with the F-4 and then contacted the center and requested radar vectors to the F-4, which we received. The join up went smoothly and I transferred the flight lead to the F-4. The en route weather was nice; we were between a high thin cirrus and a low deck of cumulus clouds.

From Phan Rang, we had traveled close to 1,000 nm in close to two hours, 15 minutes and were now within 75 nm of Taipei. Lead contacted Taipei and rocked us into close fingertip formation for the let down to initial for an overhead VFR pattern. Approaching our turn to initial, Lead dipped his wing to the left signaling three, who was on the right wing, to cross under into a left echelon formation. He cut it close, barely giving us time to stabilize in position when he had to start the turn at initial. The plane felt sluggish in the turn so I quickly checked our airspeed and saw the F-4 had us down close to 230 KIAS. I keyed the mic and said, "Push it up to 300 Lead"! Reacting to my call, he pushed it up rapidly and almost screwed up our formation with the F-4 accelerating much faster than the Hun. He momentarily got out in front where my nose was barely lined up with his tail but Number three and I caught up and were in good position by the time we pitched out over the field. If its one thing fighter pilots take pride in, it's looking good in the overhead pattern!

On the ground, the F-4 pilot, a young Lieutenant with a Major Weapons Systems Officer (WSO) in his rear seat, said, "Sorry about that. I didn't know what you guys flew initial at. Didn't realize it was that fast"! I told him no problem, thanked him for getting us there and we said our goodbyes and parted ways.

Chapter 8: The Loss of "Thunder Chicken"

At the beginning of November 1970, I already had my next assignment which was back again to F-105's at McConnell AFB, Kansas. I only had two weeks remaining at Phan Rang and I was taking in a movie at the base theater when I heard my name called out, "Is there a Major Victor Vizcarra in the house? You are wanted in the Command Post". I could not imagine what this could be about but I knew it couldn't be good.

I reported to the Command Post and a group of the Wing hierarchy was in serious discussion. When they saw me, the first thing I heard was, "Thunder Chicken just crashed short of the runway." I was just going to ask the status of the pilot when the Deputy Commander of Operations (DCO) beat me to it and added, "The pilot appears to be okay, he is at the hospital being checked." The Wing Commander then added that we needed to form an investigation board. All of a sudden, it looked like I was going to be busier these next two weeks than my whole entire time I'd been at Phan Rang. One of the first thoughts that selfishly came to mind was the possibility of being extended past my departure date! My boss acknowledged the Wing Commander's instruction about forming an investigation board and excused himself and me saying we needed to go to the safety office and review the applicable regulations regarding accident boards to make sure we didn't miss anything.

I didn't know much about accident investigation boards; luckily, my boss was an experienced safety officer, had taken me in under his wing, and was mentoring me. He was the Lt. Col flying on the wing of the Lieutenant who crashed doing the unauthorized barrel roll showing off at a remote Army camp the first month we were both here. The accident certainly was not an auspicious start for the Lt. Col projected to become the Wing Flying Safety Officer. He already knew his chances for advancement were slim to none. He had already been passed over for full Colonel once and being a Wing Safety Officer certainly wasn't a stepping-stone towards promotion. Still, he was a very dedicated officer always guiding and offering me ideas to make the safety office and me look good. He stayed in the shadows always giving me credit for ideas he had originated. It was obvious he did not want me to become stagnated in the safety field and end up like him in a dead end career. I respected him; he was not like some officers I'd seen in similar shoes whose attitude was if I'm not getting promoted, nobody under me is getting promoted.

Once in our safety office, he started tasking the ground safety Lieutenant and me with necessary actions needed to form the accident investigation board. By the next day, we had names of individuals lined up against the different board positions including a message to be sent asking for a Board President from outside the base. The Lt. Col made me the investigating officer, a position I didn't know anything about, or know how to do. I expressed my concern and he let me know the title of investigating officer sounded much more important than it really was. The job of investigating the accident was really the whole board's responsibility; my job was just to make sure they had everything they needed to do the investigation. Basically, I was little more than a gofer who was supposed to keep the board on track, something pretty hard to screw up; my boss knew exactly what he was doing, he was taking care of me.

"Thunder Chicken" was the best known most popular F-100 on the whole base; everyone knew who she was. Her name was proudly painted on her nose and she had the premiere revetment right next to the tower. Whoever was flying her knew to use her name when calling for taxi rather than the flight call sign. The tower people would respectfully

(Phan Rang Website Photo)
Thunder Chicken, Most Popular F-100 on Phan Rang.

address her by name, "Thunder Chicken, you're clear to taxi, runway 04". She was the base mascot. Now she was no more. Radio headsets would never perk up again for there would be no more calls "Thunder Chicken, ready for taxi with three chicks"; so sad. Luckily, her last pilot had survived.

As inexperienced as I was when it came to conducting an accident board, I found it unfathomable that higher headquarters would send a C-7 Caribou Lt. Col to be the board president of an F-100 accident. Surely they could have found a Lt. Col or Colonel at several of the other F-100 bases within South Vietnam. Great! Now we had an Accident Board President who didn't know a thing about F-100s and an F-100 Investigating Officer that didn't know a thing about accident boards! Talk about the non-dynamic duo!

(David McGaughey Photo)

**The Remains of Thunder Chicken
After Landing Half a Mile Short at Night.**

(David McGaughey Photo)
**Side View Showing Destruction to Thunder Chicken
And Closeness of the Damage to the Cockpit.**

(Phan Rang Website Photos)
Thunder Chicken on Crash Recovery Trailer Back at Base.

The first thing the board did after impounding aircraft maintenance and pilot records was to visit and measure the distance to the crash site. The crash recovery crew was already in place with its equipment and had made the wreckage safe for removal. They were just waiting for clearance from the board to move the aircraft to a secure hangar on the flight line. Before releasing the aircraft to the recovery crew, we had the base photographer take pictures and document the crash site. Examination of aircraft maintenance records and inspections of aircraft systems, in particular, the engine, found no discrepancies or failures; quickly ruling out any aircraft mechanical causes for the accident. A similar examination of base records verified the taxi and runway lights were on and operational, including the Visual Approach Slope Indicator (VASI) lights (A landing aid system of two sets of lights: When the pilot sees the first set white and the next set above it red, he is on the proper glide slope; both sets of lights white, you are too high; both sets of lights red, you're too low). The board shifted their attention to the pilot, first reading his statement and then interviewing him. He insisted the landing approach was normal and that he was surprised when he struck the ground as he added power to fly the aircraft up to the runway. He was very vague on the VASI's when questioned if he was using them. After he was excused, there were prolonged discussions among the board members, each giving their views of what most likely happened. The conversation centered on the timing of when the pilot recognized the need for more power and the rate at which he advanced the throttle. When the F-100 pilot board member was making a point about advancing the throttle, he used his left hand on an imaginary throttle and was moving it imitating the accident pilot's movements. I found it amusing when the Board President suggested a different movement rate; he imitated the movement using his right hand raised up to imaginary throttles on an overhead panel, slowly wiggling his hand walking the throttles typical of a C-7 multi-engine pilot!

As deliberations continued, it appeared the board was leaning more and more towards pilot error. The board flight surgeon was the only member not thinking that way. He began discussing physiological effects that may have been a contributing factor to the accident. But his discussions did not change the other members' opinions and he became the minority voice in the group.

Meanwhile, I started finding notes at my desk that the Wing Commander wanted to see me at my convenience. Finally, I broke away from one of the group's discussions that was not making any progress towards coming to a unanimous decision. I reported to the Wing Commander's office. He asked how the investigation was going and I let him know it probably was going to end up being pilot error with a possible contributing cause of physiological effects presented in a minority report by the flight surgeon. He asked me to keep him apprised, especially if anything changed. It was a very cordial meeting with good face time for me.

The very next night, I flew my last Night Owl mission of my tour. I concentrated on the recovery and tried to take in all the physiological effects the flight surgeon had been arguing as I approached the runway and landed; I was not convinced.

Upon taxiing in and shutting down, the crew chief quickly climbed up the ladder and said mobile had called saying I had struck the tailskid on landing and should check it for damage. This baffled me as I felt my landing was one of my better ones I'd had at night. I climbed down the ladder and immediately went and checked the tailskid with the crew chief. I looked at it and then turned to the crew chief and smiled. It was perfect with the very bottom of it nice and shiny from having the usual grime and dirt scraped clean by the strike on the runway. I called mobile to report there was no damage and they informed me the Wing Commander had been in mobile observing landings when I scraped the tailskid lighting up the tail area with sparks all over the bottom of the aircraft and the runway. At night, the sparks make the contact look much worse than it really is. They let me know the Wing Commander was the one who ordered them to call the crew chief to have the pilot check the skid. They also told him I was the pilot which they got from a log of the flying schedule when he asked who was the pilot.

Oh-oh, I knew I was probably going to get a call tomorrow morning to come see the Wing Commander! There went the previous day's good face time.

Sure enough, the call came in the next day for me to report to the Wing Commander's Office. Before reporting, I recalled something about tailskid strikes in the Dash-1 (Pilot's Hand Book) and I wanted to check it in preparation for the meeting. Having enough face time with the Wing Commander lately, I thought I was starting to be able to read him. But that morning, I was not sure of his mood. He started off asking, "What happened last night? That looked like a pretty bad landing". I responded, "Sir, I'm sure it must have looked much worse than it really was with all the sparks, but there was no damage to the tail end nor the tail skid. The bottom of the skid just got scraped nice and clean". I was prepared to quote the Dash-1 and I did; "Occasional contact of the tail skid is to be expected when the airplane is operated in the prescribed manner". I continued, "With all due respect sir, I was operating as the Dash-1 prescribes". The Commander, stared at me momentarily, then just gave a small shoulder shrug as he said, "Huh".

The Commander continued the meeting, "Based upon what you saw last night, do you think there is anything to this physiological theory the flight surgeon is pushing?" I told him I really didn't see it, I thought the pilot just screwed up. He nodded in agreement and said, "Okay, that'll be all".

From the Commander's office I went back to the accident board and joined-in on their deliberations. I described my previous night's approach to the runway and as tactfully as possible, I mentioned to the flight surgeon I just didn't see his theory of physiological effects being a contributing factor in the accident. Even though several of the board members nodded in agreement with me, the flight surgeon was more adamant about stating his position and submitting a minority report if the rest of the board did not agree.

Over the next few days, we wrote the final accident report with pilot error being the cause of the accident. The report listed two major factors: 1) The pilot's initial failure to recognize he was below the proper glide slope too low for a safe landing and, 2) The pilot's failure to apply power rapidly enough to arrest the aircraft's descent and prevent the aircraft from striking the ground short of the approach end overrun.

The flight surgeon, sticking to his guns, submitted a minority report as part of the final report, listing physiological factors as a contributing cause. Specific factors listed were: inadequate visual cues and insufficient lighting in dark conditions affecting pilot's sensory ability to properly determine his position relative to a proper glide slope.

Both the DCO and Wing Commander signed the report concurring with the board's findings but non-concurrence with the minority report and forwarded it to higher headquarters. I rotated back to the states before the Wing received final disposition so never learned the final outcome. I wish I could have taken the flight surgeon up on a night flight so he could have experienced approach and landing Phan Rang night conditions and maybe I could have convinced him to forego his minority report. He was a dedicated officer who firmly believed in his findings but the DCO's and Wing Commander's non-concurrence made him look bad.

Chapter 9: Saying Goodbye to the Hun

When I first in-processed into the 35th Tac Fighter Wing, my assignment started with the excellent news that I would serve only 186 days at Phan Rang instead of a full year. My year tour had been reduced by the 179 days I had previously served in Southeast Asia flying the F-105. On 11 November 1970, I flew my last F-100 flight, 182 days after having arrived at Phan Rang. It certainly had been an interesting six plus months, experiencing many new aspects of the war among them, almost daily rocket attacks. Phan Rang had the reputation of being hit the most often, albeit not the heaviest (Da Nang was the heaviest hit), than any other USAF base in South Vietnam. Sometimes, the base defense system would detect the incoming rocket and the base siren would provide a few seconds warning before the rocket struck. Other times, you'd just hear the dull but loud thump of the rocket hitting the ground. The attacks were more of a nuisance, seldom hitting anything but dirt. A rocket did hit near the squadron barracks the day I arrived and again the last day I was at Phan Rang.

In addition to dodging almost daily rockets, we had to watch out for occasional ground fire coming from outside the base perimeter during the landing pattern at night. The tower was good about issuing warnings when this occurred. Some of the pilots thought it was some of the South Korean troops guarding Phan Rang and that they were not really trying to hit us. Nonetheless, it was disconcerting!

In the previous 181 days, I had flown 119 combat missions and accumulated 213.5 hours. I reported in as a Captain and finally got to pin on Major about halfway through my tour. I had hurled my body at the ground at night more than I wished, played more poker than ever, flown a combat mission in an Aussie Canberra, and had made many great new friends. Now I was getting ready for my last F-100 mission, exciting but at the same time, a little remorseful. I thought of the aviation saying, "It is better to walk out to your plane knowing this is your last flight than walk out to your plane not knowing this is your last flight".

I was scheduled for a morning mission with Doug Lea from the 615th TFS to fly our end of tour flights together. We took off and headed north for a rendezvous with a FAC. Typically, the morning clouds were already starting to build to the towering cumulonimbus of afternoon thunderstorms. Everything was proceeding normal until we changed radio frequency to contact the FAC. When I went to check in on the new frequency, the radio was dead. After a couple of unsuccessful attempts to transmit, I signaled Doug we needed to go back to our previous frequency. Doing that did not cure the problem; I had an inoperative radio. Being our last mission, Doug didn't want to have to air abort.

I watched as Doug went through some wild gyrations in the cockpit and finally ended up holding his emergency radio he had retrieved from his survival vest. I had to hand it to him for his ingenuity and dedication to getting the mission done. It probably really wasn't as difficult or challenging as it appeared, but embarrassingly, close to seven months of being the Wing's flying safety conscience trumpeted my fighter pilot willingness to take it to the edge. My first thought was, "and the Major lost control of his aircraft how? Well sir, instead of his hand being on the control stick, it was momentarily entangled between his parachute chest strap, seat harness, and survival vest"! Looking at Doug, I shook my head no!

If I had it to do all over again, I would have gone to all that trouble and more to be able to complete that mission. Unfortunately, we seldom get second chances in aviation. Without me being able to communicate with any other aircraft or ground controller (including the FAC), we had to abort the mission. In retrospect, we could have had Doug deliver his ordnance under FAC control while I held high and dry. Instead, we flew out over the ocean and jettisoned our bombs.

Doug kept some semblance of an aggrandized last flight by leading us to an overhead VFR pattern instead of chasing me in a straight in approach and landing because of my radio being out. That would have been extremely anti-climatic for an end of tour flight. Turning initial for the overhead pattern, Doug informed the tower I was NORDO (no radio) and to clear me to land with a green light. At least we were able to look good with a nice tight formation on initial, sharp break, and relative tight landing pattern, all observed by the greeting party waiting on the ramp.

A couple of our squadron mates intercepted us on motorcycles as we taxied onto the de-arming area. The riders wearing bandoleers and army helmets strapped flares on the back of their cycles which they popped and escorted us zigzagging along the taxiway with trailing orange smoke as we taxied back to the ramp.

It's an Air Force tradition for pilots to get wetted down on their last flights. Doug and I had agreed to wait for each other after parking and deplane together so we could charge whoever had the water hose and capture it. We each were handed a bottle of champagne before we even got out of the cockpit. I got hit by a stream of water while climbing down the ladder, ran over and shook Doug's hand, and then we both put our bottles of champagne on the ramp and charged the individual with the water hose. The three of us ended up being completely soaked by the time we finally were able to turn the nozzle off to the amusement of the greeting party. We were honored to have the top brass join the celebration on the ramp adding their congratulations on completing our tours.

(Personal Photo)
End of Tour Greeting Party.

Doug was an excellent pilot and a very likable guy, always with a smile and twinkle in his eye. Little did I know when we parted ways on the ramp that day, that 17 months later, we would be flying together again instructing foreign students in the F-5.

(Personal Photo)
Parking the Old Hun for the Last Time, 11 November 1970

(Personal Photo)
Fini

That evening, the squadron threw me a great going away party. I packed and processed out over the next two days in preparation of departing South Vietnam on 14 November 1970.

I had now experienced the Vietnam War, both in the North and in the South. The lethality of AAA, SAM's and MiG's over the skies of North Vietnam required totally different combat tactics than operations in the South. The threat environment in the South did not have these types of weapons making it possible to employ low altitude weapons delivery with relative low risk. The chances of getting shot down in an F-100 in the South were six times less than an F-105 over the North. However, this did not mean flying missions in the South was a piece of cake. There were many examples of hairy F-100 missions flown under the most dangerous conditions and critical timing.

Such was the case on the evening of 6 August, 1967 when 1,500 NVA regulars attacked the army camp at Tong Le Chon, 80 nm NW of Saigon. Eight Green Berets quickly found themselves deserted by the 400 "Chieli Hoi" (Repatriated Viet Cong) assigned to the camp. A FAC put out a call on Guard frequency for air support from any airborne fighter in the area. Lt. Col. Kenneth Miles, Commander of the 614th Tac Fighter Squadron at Phan Rang happened to be airborne with his wingman and answered the FAC's urgent radio message. When briefed the conditions, Miles informed the FAC that the reported weather of an 800-foot ragged ceiling and the camp's location in between hills and rapidly rising mountainous terrain on both sides ruled out their ability to get into the area and provide the required air support. The FAC pleaded for help stating eight Green Berets were about to die!

Miles asked JO Hanford, his wingman, "Well JO, want to give it a try JO?" JO responded, "Sure Boss, lets go" and joined on lead's wing for a weather penetration. In a dangerous and daring feat, Miles used a TACAN radial and distance cut and penetrated the weather hoping he would be in the center of the narrow valley when they'd popped out underneath the low ceiling.

As they broke out under the weather, Miles thought he could make out the triangular outline of the camp at 12 o'clock and proceeded to drop a napalm can in front of the entry to the outpost. With the burning napalm lighting up the narrow valley, the two F-100's set up a pattern and continued to make multiple passes at the masses of enemy troops trying to breach the camp walls, bombing and strafing until they were "Winchester" (out of ammo). Their repeated attacks had put a temporary stop to the assault with many of the enemy retreating away from the camp perimeter. Departing, Miles told the FAC they were going back to reload and that they would be back ASAP.

Upon landing at Phan Rang, Miles and his wingman jumped out of their jets and climbed into two newly loaded F-100s. They returned to the camp where the attack had resumed. It was now between 2 and 3 AM, apparently the NVA had not expected their return and quickly dispersed and retreated back into the jungle once the F-100's started doing multiple passes again. Miles and JO were credited with saving the camp and more importantly, the lives of eight Green Berets, seven of whom had fought off the invaders while gravely wounded.

On 14 November, my boss surprised me, continuing to take care of me and arranged for my own private flight in an O-2 to Cam Ranh Bay AB to catch the "Freedom Bird," instead of having to fly up in a regularly scheduled C-123 run.

(Personal Photo)
Catching an O-2 Flight to Cam Ranh Bay AB

(Personal Photo)
Getting Briefed by the O-2 Pilot.

(Personal Photo)
Goodbye to the Hun and Phan Rang.

Although there were several close calls with too many tree strikes, there were no losses due to enemy shoot downs during my near seven-month tour. On my flight in the O-2 to catch the "Freedom Bird", I was pleased with the thought I was not leaving any friends or acquaintances behind as casualties of the war like I had during my Thud tours over the North.

Regrettably, 15 days after my private flight to Cam Ranh Bay, the C-123 taking passengers to catch their "Freedom Bird" crashed in fog and rain into a mountain ridge 15 miles south of Cam Ranh killing 42, three of which were 35th Wing F-100 pilots who had just completed their combat tours. So close, yet so far!

Chapter 10: "Sing it Again Sam"

    I met Sam Morgan in early 1964 when I got assigned to F-105's in the 80th Tac Fighter Squadron, Itazuke AB, Fukuoka, Japan. Sam was a free-spirited young bachelor who had been in the 35th Tac Fighter Squadron, a sister Squadron, since arriving in 1960. He elected to extend past his original date of return to the states (DOROS) and made the transition from F-100's to the F-105. Sam was well known for pushing the envelope with "Bart" Barthelmas and several other bachelor icons who were the epitome of the fighter pilot spirit. "Bart", unfortunately, was killed in action (KIA) in the first counter strike against SAM sites in North Vietnam, 27 July 1965, during "Operation Spring High".

    Sam is a great story teller who would every once in awhile ask, "Did I ever tell you about the time…" and then proceed to entertain you with some great tale, some hilarious, others which could only elicit a large "Wow!" A great friend and fighter pilot, he has been kind enough to provide me the following experiences from his F-100 days.

(USAF Photo)
Sam Morgan F-100 "Hero Picture".

USAF Photo)
William "Bart" Barthelmas Sam Morgan's Partner in Crime.

T-33 Bailout

Sometime in 1960 or 61 we were having a large number of F-100 crashes at all of the bases -- Itazuke, Misawa, Okinawa, Clark, Taiwan. Later it was found that the Wiggings hydraulic disconnect between the tail and the forward part of the bird were failing and causing a hydraulic lockup of the stabilizer. Before that was discovered, other measures were taken to reduce crashes and one was to prohibit a pilot being an Element Lead until he had 650-hours of operational time.

A number of us had Element Lead status until this ruling and we were immediately removed from that status which was an aggravation, especially since we all felt that very few of the crashes were due to pilot error. Marty Case came up with a "skull & crossbones" patch that we wore on a lower sleeve. At 500-hours we got a star on top of the patch and at 650-hours we got a wreath around the star -- much like the Senior and Command Pilot wings.

It didn't matter what type of aircraft the time was in. I found out that there was a T-33 flight out of base ops at first light each morning. This flight was to weather recce the ranges and the area. It was normally flown with an empty back seat that was available most of the time to any pilot who asked for the ride. I decided to check this out. I don't remember the pilots name but he said he would be glad to have me ride along.

At that time, there was very little weather information available except for terminal conditions at the bases. Also communications between bases was spotty at best. Just calling from Itazuke to Osan was a challenge that required a call to the command post to make several links and these links were such that after each comment you had to say "over" so the people in the link knew to switch the signal. So, when we took off in the T-33 we knew the weather was bad at Itazuke and little more.

We climbed out in the weather and headed toward the Ashia Gunnery Range. Radar was guiding us to the range and the pilot let down to 2,000 feet where we were still in the clouds. The pilot announced that the range was closed in by weather and pushed up the power for a climb when there was a loud explosion from the engine. Something came through the console on my left and heavy smoke started coming through the opening. The engine was still running but barely and there was severe vibration in the entire aircraft.

The pilot said that we would go back over the land and punch out. I told him the range was surrounded by mountains. He said, "Okay, when the canopy goes, follow it out". He then raised the canopy electrically and it did not come off. I now had this large air scoop and I was really getting beat by the wind. Also the T-33 had an instrument hood that covered the back canopy and was held by bungee cords running the length of the back canopy. I was covered by that hood and all of those bungees. It seemed like a very long time before the canopy finally separated but, when it did, I pulled the handles and squeezed the triggers.

It was the old seat with just a cannon shell to get you out and it did the job. I was struck by the violence and noise of the wind and the damaged airplane were suddenly gone - I was tumbling in the clouds in total silence. And I noticed that the chute was not open and I knew I was low.

I checked and the D-ring was gone. It was a backpack and I reached back and could feel it was open. I started shaking the cords when I came out of the bottom of the clouds face down at less than traffic pattern altitude. Suddenly the chute caught, I got one or two swings and landed in a plowed field. A very old Japanese woman was in the field and she came up and handed me a grapefruit. I gave her the whistle from the survival pack.

I could hear a Gooney Bird circling in the clouds but we didn't have radios then so I knew there was nothing he or I could do. A Japanese on a motorcycle offered to take me off the mountain to Ashia AB, so I hopped on. At Ashia, I found both the T-33 and the C-47 on the ground.

As I was coming out in the seat the T-33 came out of the clouds right over Ashia AB and the pilot dead sticked it in. The T-33 had a centrifugal compressor and it had lost a chunk of metal that came up through my left console -- hence the engine failure. I got a ride back to Itazuke in the Gooney Bird. Willie Wilson met me at Base Ops and said, "Glad you made it".

The next day Milt Songy and I drove back up to Ashia and picked up the survival gear that I couldn't carry on the motorcycle.

I remember my back hurt a bit at the time and that has never changed. I didn't say anything at the time because I did not want to be put on Duty Not Involving Flying (DNIF) status but it continued to be an aggravation. When I got to McConnell AFB, KS, I got some treatment for it but nothing useful. For years now I have had an 800-mg Ibuprofen prescription to manage this problem.

Taking Out the Power Lines at Pyong Tech, Korea

I think it was 1962 or maybe 61 and we were 1st Lieutenants. Bart and I were sent to Osan, Korea, in an F-100F as an Armed Forces Day static display. We had the night off so we took a taxi to Pyong Tech for an evening at the Officers' Club. We were carrying on at the bar, eating a raw steak, and yelling & hollering. There were a bunch of Koran girls in the room wearing evening dresses and Bart kept yelling, "What are these wh... doing in the O Club? Finally, some Colonel came up and announced he was in charge of the Post and he had as much of us as he could stand. He was in the process of heaving us out when another Colonel came up, announced he was in charge of the helicopter unit, and he wanted us to stay. We stayed and I don't remember how the evening ended but we awoke in a tent the next morning with a Sergeant shinning our shoes (you had to wear Class A off base in Korea). He said we had made a hit the night before and there was a helicopter waiting to take us wherever we wanted. We did not feel well so we opted for a ride back to Osan.

We flipped a coin and I lost so Bart went to the Alert Pad and to bed and I went to the flight line to stand static display with the airplane. About mid afternoon, Bart came bopping down, fresh as a daisy, and said, "Let's go". I told him we had to stay till 1700 and he said, "Bull shit". We climbed in, cranked, tossed the ladder off onto the ramp, and started taxiing through the crowd -- me in the back and Bart in the front. We had 450-gallon external tanks so lots of fuel but a 450-knot speed limit. As we climbed out Bart said, "We can't go back without saying goodbye to our Army friends" and I said, "course not". We were at about 20,000 and below us we could see hundreds of tents in very neat rows and columns with a broad main street right down the middle -- all dirt roads. Bart nosed over with the burner lit and headed down. I told him we were over the tank limit and he said he didn't worry about that. Soon we are very low and at a very high speed coming down main street. To give you an idea of the altitude, we almost made it under the wires -- but not quite. We hit and I hollered that we had hit something. Bart said he didn't feel it. I told him to look back at my canopy where it was scratched opaque except for two little bands, one on each side. I could see damage to the tanks. Bart pulled up and we headed for Japan. He suggested that we go out over the Sea of Japan, bail out, and claim that it caught fire. I vetoed that idea and told him they would know why it caught fire. We landed at Itazuke after dark on a Friday night so the only person on the flight line was a guy to set the chocks. When we got out of the aircraft he said something to the effect, " Holy Shit! What did you guys hit?" We told him to put the bird in the hanger, we would be back.

Our Maintenance Officer was Captain Mother Hubbard and we had squadron maintenance. We went to the club, got Mother, and returned to the hanger. As we walked in he said something to the effect, "Holy Shit, what did you guys hit?" We told him we had already gone through that with the mechanic, could we fix it?

We worked with the mechanics all weekend putting on a new canopy, new tanks, and some skin patching on the rudder, which was what cut the wires. On Monday, things seemed quiet so at 1400, Bart came up and suggested we go to the club to celebrate the Great Escape. We were at the bar celebrating when Colonel Max Bell came in, ordered us to attention, and read Article 32 of the UCMJ (Anything you say can......). It turns out we had not noticed the skin missing on top of the nose. Charlie McClarren had gone out to fly the plane and as he topped the ladder, he glanced at the nose to see nothing but ribs and radios. Later we wire brushed him a bit for being a snitch.

We were grounded and the investigation started. Many times I was asked if I was innocent and I had to say we were both equally guilty although I probably would have gotten under the wires. After about a month where I was permanent range officer and Bart (I think) was permanent Mobile, they had a big trial -- like a real criminal trial. After deliberations they announced that it wasn't really our fault but it was a lack of training; that indeed, with the right training we would have made it under the wires. They started with the punishment phase and were starting to say that Bart and I could not fly together for a month when our Flight Commander, Bob Middlebrooks, hopped up from the back and said, "Hold it Colonel, I think you are being too hard on the boys." Bart then hopped up and told Middlebrooks to be quiet. After a little discussion the court agreed and announced that we would take a low level training mission to Korea with Middlebrooks in the back as the Instructor.

The Army never complained.

Another Day on the Alert Pad in C-Diamond at Osan AB, Korea

The Thursday crew-change was past, we had watched all five movies, we were bored, and the Alert Bell sounded for a scramble. It was a choreographed exercise where the pilots and mechanics headed for the aircraft, strapped in, started the engines, and waited for the codes. The codes didn't come and it was announced that it was the daily exercise.

The F-100s were loaded with the old fission bombs, the bombs with the fissionable material looking like a small bowling ball on the end of a screw jack. The pilot had a panel where he could operate the jack to run the ball into the rest of the bomb, which then made it an Atomic Bomb. The rules were there for nuclear weapons but it was a fairly new business for fighter pilots. I remember one of the pilots complaining that it was taking longer that normal for his bomb to insert the ball. The Alert Pad Commander threw a fit and told the pilot he was not supposed to be inserting the ball on the Pad.

Being that the aircraft were nuclear loaded, the two-man concept was demanded. Anytime any person had access to the aircraft, there had to be two trained persons present and this was usually the pilot and the mechanic. This was a bit problematic since each shelter had two birds and hence two bombs but only one Security Guard when the pilots and mechanics were absent. So, most of the time, there was only the Security Guard alone in the shelter with two F-100 aircraft loaded with an Atomic Bomb.

I always marveled at the endurance of the guards. They worked a 13-hour night shift and an 11-hour day shift. Korean winters are bitterly cold with strong winds. These guards stood for 13-hours in bitter, bitter cold alone in an open aircraft shelter. I do not know how they survived.

Anyway the exercise was over so it was time to top off the fuel in the aircraft, check system air pressures, and button up for the next scramble. My Crew Chief announced that I had a low nose tire that he would have to air-up.

Tires on an aircraft are different from automobile tires in many ways. They are much, much more rigid so you don't just roll them onto the rims. For the F-100 the sides of the rims separated after a ring of bolts were removed. The tire people would put half the rim on each side of the tire and then bolt the halves together. I think the main tires had 250 psi and the two nose tires had 150 psi each. So my Crew Chief was going to get an air compressor and add air to my nose wheel tires.

There were two types of air compressors – the High Pacs and the Low Pacs. The High Pacs would go to 3,000 psi, which for air pressure, is a very big number. I used to fill my SCUBA tanks with a High Pac and it took a full hour to fill one tank to 2,200 psi.

The compressors were few and probably half the alert birds needed some kind of air charge so we were waiting for a compressor to be brought to us. The other pilot in the shelter with me was Tim Ogle and we were standing at his bird chatting while waiting for the birds to be serviced. The pilots had to be in the shelter to meet the Two-Man requirement for the bomb but we had no responsibilities while the birds were being serviced. I was leaning on his refueling probe and he was leaning against the wing root when there was an enormous explosion at my bird.

I turned to see my Crew Chief holding a very bloody leg saying something like "the valve failed". He didn't want to wait for a Low Pac so he tried to air the tire with a High Pac. He was trying to meter in 150 psi when the valve failed and the full 3,000 psi went to the tire. The rim separated and shot between Tim and me and smashed the side of his aircraft. The bolts holding the rim had failed and the nuts that failed made a string of holes in Tim's plane, which looked like it had been raked by machine gun fire.

For a few moments there was total chaos as it was a startling event but then people went into action. I ran to the dispatch truck in front of the shelter and told him to call for an ambulance and a fire truck. There was no fire but there was a lot of jet fuel, two Atomic Bombs, and two damaged aircraft. Tim went to the Crew Chief and helped him to the ground. Within seconds the emergency vehicles arrived and the Chief was off in the ambulance.

As just a 1st. Lieutenant pilot I was spared most of the drama that followed. It had to be a Broken Spear, which was an enormous problem. We had two birds off alert and replacements had to be brought in and staged for alert. Tim and I had to be with the new birds until they were set for alert.

It was not the ordinary day on the Alert Pad.

I Did Not Boom Fukuoka

One of my first duties after arriving at Itazuke in September 1960 was "Paymaster". I had to go to finance to pick up a large bag of money and a pay list. I then set up a table and every military member, officer and enlisted, had to come to the table for their pay. Most of them saluted, signed their line on the list, and I gave them an envelope with the right amount of Script inside. I did the envelopes to ensure I had the money counted right since I was told that I had to pay any shortages.

Shortly after that the AF went to checks so the Paymaster simply had to pass out the checks with no cash involved.

On Friday afternoon, fairly late, Bobby Mead called me in and said I had to take the checks to Korea; I was the Paymaster for the Osan members of the wing. It was to be a big night at the club so I protested with great agony but Bobby simply said, "You are not being asked to volunteer". I said "Okay" and asked for a clean F-100D for the trip. It wasn't legal but I called Don Majors on the PAD and asked him to pick up and distribute the checks. The Paymaster was never to delegate responsibilities but I trusted Shakey Majors.

I landed at Osan just as it was getting dark and had the bird turned while I ran to Diamond C to give Shakey the checks. When I got back to the bird it was ready so I cranked and taxied. It was dark when I pulled onto the runway and took off. I think I was the only guy up in that part of the world as it was clear, dark, and quiet. As I approached Pusan I was talking with the radar site above Itazuke and the controller told me I was moving at almost 1,000 kts over the ground meaning I was right in the jet stream. I told him I was going to turn at Pusan and kick it up to max speed and I wanted a speed check. He said he would try but, at that speed, he would get only four sweeps coming across to Japan.

My plan was to go to the ADF on Ikashema Island at max speed and make a circle in idle and boards to get subsonic before the let down to Itazuke. I was really screaming across the Straights when Approach Control broke in to tell me I needed to make a straight in descent to Itazuke from present position. I dropped to idle and boards (speed brakes) and pointed the nose toward the lights of Fukuoka which were over 50-miles away. Things seemed to go well as I was soon on the ground and heading for the Top of the Mach Club (Officer's Club).

When I arrived at the club, there were about 50-guys standing outside, led by Willie Wilson, cheering and clapping. I must have looked puzzled so Willie runs up and tells me that was the loudest sonic boom he had ever heard. I could only think "Oh shit".

And indeed it started the next morning. I met most everyone on the base in a senior position the next morning for questions about "what I had done". Then in the afternoon the complaints from the Japanese in the area and the staff at 5AF started calling. I feigned innocence and suggested that it had to be the marines some distance north of us. I was told there were no marines airborne and that only me and our Wing Commander Col. George Daniels were airborne. I think a couple of times I might have suggested that it might have been Colonel Daniels and that didn't sell. Bobby Mead the ops officer said I needed to hide so he sent me to Osan for two weeks.

While at Osan I got a call that I needed to send a written message back to Itazuke stating that I did or did not boom Fukuoka. I thought about that a lot as I worried about a false official statement but finally rationalized that I really didn't boom Fukuoka as I was subsonic 50-miles away; I was guilty of nothing more than a very high speed run from Korea. So I sent a message back saying, "I did not boom Fukuoka". Somewhere I have a copy of that message tucked away.

Well for the two weeks at Osan I didn't hear much more so I thought things were quieting down a bit. But when I got back home I was told I was the permanent Range Officer at Ashia Range. I had a new Colt Python 357 so I rounded up a case of 38-special, hopped on my new Honda Superhawk motorcycle, and went to the Range. I had been there a week and was running low on ammo when I got a call to close the range and report to the Wing Commander. Again, I thought "Oh shit".

I motorcycled to the Suenaga House (off base Japanese house a group of bachelors rented) and suited up in Class A and went to Colonel Daniel's office. The secretary told me he wanted me sitting right out side his office. It was probably close to noon or a bit earlier.

I sat there till almost 1800 hours without talking with anyone. I could see Col Daniels coming and going but as it got later, most of the lights were turned off and everyone left but me and Col. Daniels. Finally he stepped out and said, "Sam, come on in". As I walked in and started to salute, he turned and picked up a bolt of blue material and set it on his desk. He said this was the material for the new Class A and, if I wanted to have a suit made, he would be glad to sell me some. I mumbled something about how I would love to have a new uniform. He said fine, let him how much I wanted. Then he smiled real big and said, "Don't worry about that sonic boom business, I think we have it taken care of". I saluted and left thinking all the while, "What just happened"?

I did get back from Korea in time for the Friday event, I did get extra time in Korea, I did get a lot of Range Officer time, but I survived!

Old Taylor (Not an Itazuke story, but it is an F-100 story.)

I was in F-100 training at Williams AFB, AZ in the fall of 1959 when I came down with "Valley Fever". Valley Fever is like a really bad case of flu with emphasis on upper respiratory problems. It was bad enough that I was too hoarse to talk so my Flight Commander sent me to the hospital where I was admitted.

This was 1959 and the hospital was a WW II remnant, a big open bay area with half a dozen or so beds lined up along each side. It was late evening when a lot of activity started and I hear a F-100 had gone in short of the runway. Sometime later a guy was wheeled in that was literally burnt to a crisp.

I don't mean to exaggerate about his burns but he was black. I grew up in Bluefield, WV, the heart of the Pocahontas coal country, just up from the Tug River of the Hatfield-McCoy stories, just a short distance from Bloody Thurmond and I have seen men come out of the mines black. But this guy was totally black and looked like a body-shaped lump of coal.

The next morning as it was just getting daylight I went down to the bed where the pilot was lying and he was awake, groaning, and suffering. He was black all over as this was before Nomex flight suits (fire retardant flight suits) and his skin was a thick black crust – again all over his body. And it was cracked in many places with a thick yellow liquid oozing out of every crack. He looked dreadful to say the least.

I asked him what happened and he said he landed well short of the runway. The bird rolled up in a ball of fire with him in it before he was thrown clear of the wreckage. He said he was in the grass and the fire truck had near rolled over him getting to the fire. When the fireman could not find him in the wreckage, they started looking around till they found him in the grass.

I was just making silly conversation and told him it shouldn't be long before he recovered and would be back in the air. He told me his name was Taylor and that he would never get back in another airplane – ever.

Later that day I was released and went back to the squadron where I told them about Taylor.

About seven years later I arrived at McConnell with the 561 TFS and ran into a Captain Taylor who was one of the maintenance officers. I noted his name "Taylor" and told him I had met a Taylor at Williams. He said that he was that Taylor. He looked great! He looked normal with no burn scars, he had hair, and he moved fine.

I told him what I had seen and his recovery was remarkable. I asked if he had ever flown again. He said NEVER again would he get in an airplane, which I had heard him say before. He meant it.

The Great Cross Country

I am thinking this happened in the early winter of 1963. The weather in Japan had been dreadful for at least a month and it wasn't much better in Korea. We were getting almost no flying at all and especially so with a third of the wing – 24 F-100's – on constant alert in Korea.

The wing people decided that we would send four birds from each of the three squadrons, 35 TFS, 36 TFS, and 80 TFS, on cross country with no instructions other than to fly as much as possible without coming back to Itazuke and we could not go south of Okinawa. That meant we could go to Kadena AB, Osan AB, Yokota AB, and Misawa AB. But, like I said, it was winter and you don't really want to go to Misawa in the winter.

My 35th TFS flight was composed of myself, Milt Songy, Mike Kividra, and someone I cannot remember. The 80 TFS took off first with 15-minutes between each flight of four. The birds were configured with the ferry tanks making them heavy so there would be 15-seconds between each bird in a flight taking off.

The aircraft at Itazuke were parked in a line facing the runway. Milt Songy was leading our flight on the first sortie and we had started engines. The procedures for the F-100 had the pilot and the Crew Chief go through a routine after engine start for bleeding air from the flight control hydraulic systems. The pilot stirred the control stick while the mechanic stood on the wing and opened a valve in the compartment behind the pilot.

So I am sitting in the aircraft about midfield, facing the runway, engine running and I am stirring the stick. To my right, I see the four birds from the 80 TFS pulling out on the runway, lining up, and running the engines to full military power. I see Number One release brakes and start the takeoff roll. Then, 15-seconds later Two starts his roll followed another 15-seconds by Three. Then, after another 15-seconds, Four starts his roll.

I see Four's nose come up and then the bird lifts off but it wasn't right. I see the right wing start to drop as soon as the plane leaves the ground and it keeps dropping. The bird is climbing but it looks like it is going to do a roll right after lift off. I watch the bird roll almost inverted and the nose is coming down.

The F-100 had a long pitot boom on the front of the plane and Number Four is close enough that I can clearly see the pitot boom make contact with the ground with the bird maybe 20-degrees nose down and inverted. It looked like the instant the pitot boom touched the ground the F-100 became a very large fireball.

After a few seconds of silence, my flight started talking about whether we should continue the mission. We decided we needed to check back in the squadron so we shut down and walked back to the squadron building. We were standing at the duty desk when the Ops Officer, Don McCance rushed in the door, looked at us, and with his finger pointing at us, said, "One, Two, Three, Four – Oh, I am relieved." He did not know who had died in the crash.

The bird that crashed had a history. I think it was Fred Cherry landing when the hook caught the barrier on the approach end. The barrier was nothing more than a lot of anchor chain from a very large Navy ship and it was set up to be pulled in one direction only. And it was not the direction Fred was flying when he caught the chain. The landing gear failed when Fred's bird was yanked to the ground and the wing was damaged but the plane was repairable.

The damaged F-100 was carried to Taipei, Taiwan to the IRAN (Inspect and Repair as Necessary) for repairs. We were notified that it was ready so John Atkinson (80 TFS) went down to pick it up. He said it flew fine for the return to Japan although the right wing "seemed a little heavy". This would not have been unusual and for John, it was nothing more than a nuisance.

On the day of the crash, it was flown by 1st Lieutenant Frankfather, a new guy who had recently arrived on his first assignment.

Major McCance told us to start up and press on. We did and we made it to Osan where we spent the night. The next morning, we had heavy snow with the weather being right at minimums. We wanted to go but needed clearance from the Detachment Commander, Joe Klauman. The four of us were pressing for his clearance and, with great reluctance and concern, he said okay.

We got the birds started and were heading for the runway very slowly. The F-100 had 250 psi air in the main tires so they were rock hard and braking in snow was not great. We had swapped the lead and Songy was now back in the formation. We were assembling on the runway when Songy started screaming in the radio "No Brakes". I looked back and could see him slowly moving to impale Kividra with the pitot boom and there was lots of red fluid coming out of his aircraft. He had Utility Hydraulic Failure with no brakes nor steering so he just shut off the engine. His bird stopped before it hit Kividra.

We left Songy and headed out. Over that weekend, I got over 30-hours of flying. The birds were wearing out. We left Songy in Korea and Kividra in Okinawa. The two of us still flyable were just going from Kadena to Osan to Yokota and back. About half way through the mission the wingman's radio quit working and all my outside lights failed but we would press on.

The last night we were going into Yokota and holding over Tokyo. The jet stream was so strong over Tokyo that I didn't have to fly the holding pattern. At 250-knots I was stationary over Tokyo.

Approach Control wanted to separate us for separate approaches until I told them the wingman had no radio. The controller then said that he recognized us as the two who came in the night before without a radio and he didn't want us coming back again until we got the radio fixed.

The next day we went home!

Epilogue

The F-100 was the first of four fighters I flew in my military career spanning over 24 years. After flying the Hun for sixteen months, I transitioned to the F-105, then returned to the Hun close to seven years later. My total career tactical fighter time of 2694 flight hours also included flying the F-5 and the F-4. Having flown these four classic fighters, it is very difficult to fairly assess which one I considered to be "the best". For one thing, there is a natural propensity to have a special fondness for an aircraft that you have taken into combat and has brought you home safely.

An unbiased way to objectively compare the "goodness" between two fighters is to compare their energy maneuverability diagrams. Seldom will an aircraft have better performance throughout its entire flight envelope over another aircraft of the same vintage. Normally, you will find similar era designs will have different areas in their flight envelopes in which they outperform or are at a disadvantage compared to the other aircraft. Overlaying the respective plots will reveal where in the flight envelope each aircraft is at an advantage or disadvantage.

Unfortunately, I have been unable to find comparison plots for the aircraft I flew because of their age. With more time, intensive research, or applying energy maneuverability formulas, an objective comparison is possible. So rather than expounding upon which fighter I flew was better, I'll provide a subjective opinion on what I liked about each fighter I had the pleasure of flying.

Even though all four fighters I flew were designed and developed within six years of the same decade, advancements in aeronautics, jet engine technology, and avionics put the F-100 at a disadvantage in what I liked about it compared to the later fighters.

The Hun provided a quantum leap in performance over its predecessors introducing supersonic flight and operations in flight regimes previously experienced only by experimental "X" series aircraft. The first in the century series to operate in this expanded flight envelope, the F-100 was susceptible to inertial coupling, a flight phenomena previously not experienced in aircraft design and one which was avoided in fighters that followed it. This made it a more difficult plane to fly in the 200-Kt high AOA flight regime compared to the other three fighters.

The F-5A, which first flew some six years after the F-100, was smaller in size, flew and felt very much like an F-100, but without its inherent adverse flight characteristics. It had the highest roll rate of the four fighters and was spin resistant, a flight characteristic that made it a perfect fighter for third world emerging Air Forces. I always thought of it as a "sports car" version of the Hun.

Although the F-105 was initially slated to replace the F-100 as the mainstay tactical fighter, it was designed to totally different specifications as a low altitude, high speed, tactical nuclear attack fighter. Its high wing loading gave it superior stability, especially in low altitude, high-speed turbulence. Relatively advanced for its day, multi-mode radar and integrated avionics gave the Thud a much-increased combat capability, especially in weather, over the F-100. It had the best ergonomically designed cockpit of the four fighters I flew.

The F-4 designed within five years of the F-100, surprisingly, had the adverse yaw flight characteristic of the Hun, albeit, not as drastic. I loved its power from the two J-79 engines but disliked the cockpit layout; the control stick felt like it was too low and the throttles too far back. I preferred the F-100's heavier stick feel than the F-4's relative lighter controls.

What endeared me to the F-100 was that as the first of the century series, it effectively advanced tactical operations from the golden age of early post World War II jets to the new supersonic age. Lacking automation advancements that would appear in more advanced fighters as new technology expanded exponentially, it required good old fashion pilot skills to handle several challenging characteristics of the F-100, such as adverse yaw at high AOA low speeds, high landing speeds, and the engine power curve. A difficult fighter to fly correctly, once mastered, you knew you had reached a higher plateau in being a good fighter pilot.

(Personal Photo)

From Cessna 172's to ......

(Personal Photo)

F-100D Hun Pilot

Appendix

F-100 STATISTICS

Model	1st Flight	Number Produced	Max Weight	Wing Span	Length
YF-100A	05/25/1953	2	28,561	36' 7"	46' 3"
F-100A	10/09/1953	203	28,899	38' 9"	47' 1"
F-100C	01/17/1954	476	36,549	38' 9"	47' 1"
F-100D	01/24/1956	1,274	38,048	38' 9"	47' 1"
F-100F	03/07/1957	339	39,122	38' 9"	50' 4"
Total		2,294			

Highest accident rate of any USAF fighter with 889 F-100's destroyed in accidents killing 324 pilots.

F-100 Vietnam War Statistics

- Primary fighter-bomber for South Vietnam combat operations.
- First Wild Weasel Platform, achieved first SAM site kill.
- 360,283 combat sorties flown, more than any other fighter in South Vietnam.
- Credited with one MiG-17 "probable" kill.
- 186 lost to enemy action.
- 45 lost to operational accidents.
- 7 destroyed on the ground by VC base attacks

Section I   T.O. 1F-100D-1

MAIN DIFFERENCES TABLE
F-100 SERIES

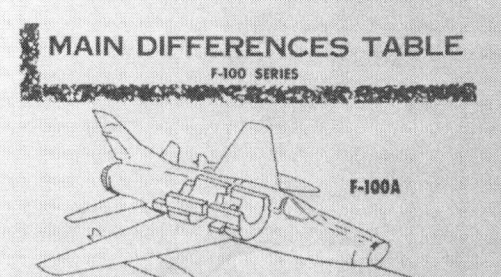

F-100A

ENGINE	J57-7, -39, -21, OR -21A WITH AFTERBURNER
AC ELECTRICAL POWER SOURCE	THREE INVERTERS
ARMAMENT	FOUR GUNS, AND ON SOME AIRPLANES, VARIOUS EXTERNAL LOADS
CAMERAS	SIGHT
DROP TANKS	TWO 275-GALLON
INTERNAL FUEL	FUSELAGE
REFUELING PROVISIONS	GRAVITY TANK FILLING
FLAPS	NO
OXYGEN SYSTEM	GASEOUS, WITH D-2 REGULATOR
AUTOPILOT	NO

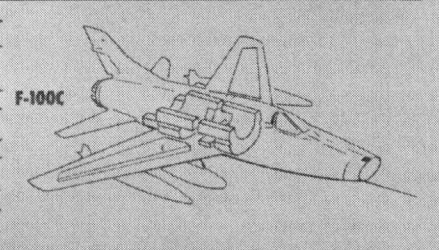

F-100C

ENGINE	J57-7, -39, -21, OR -21A WITH AFTERBURNER
AC ELECTRICAL POWER SOURCE	THREE INVERTERS
ARMAMENT	FOUR GUNS AND VARIOUS COMBINATIONS OF EXTERNAL LOADS INCLUDING BOMBS AND ROCKETS MOUNTED ON REMOVABLE PYLONS
CAMERAS	SIGHT AND STRIKE
DROP TANKS	TWO 275-GALLON AND/OR COMBINATION OF 200-GALLON (TWO 450-GALLON ON SOME AIRPLANES)
INTERNAL FUEL	FUSELAGE AND WING
REFUELING PROVISIONS	PRESSURE TYPE (SINGLE-POINT AND AIR REFUELING)
FLAPS	NO
OXYGEN SYSTEM	LIQUID, WITH D-2A REGULATOR
AUTOPILOT	NO

F-100D

ENGINE	J57-21 OR -21A WITH AFTERBURNER
AC ELECTRICAL POWER SOURCE	ONE ENGINE-DRIVEN AC GENERATOR WITH ONE STAND-BY INVERTER
ARMAMENT	FOUR GUNS AND VARIOUS COMBINATIONS OF EXTERNAL LOADS INCLUDING BOMBS AND ROCKETS (MISSILES ON SOME AIRPLANES) MOUNTED ON FORCE EJECTION PYLONS
CAMERAS	SIGHT AND STRIKE
DROP TANKS	TWO 275-GALLON AND/OR COMBINATION OF 200-GALLON (TWO 450-GALLON ON SOME AIRPLANES)
INTERNAL FUEL	FUSELAGE AND WING
REFUELING PROVISIONS	PRESSURE-TYPE (SINGLE-POINT AND AIR REFUELING)
FLAPS	YES
OXYGEN SYSTEM	LIQUID WITH MD-1 REGULATOR
AUTOPILOT	SOME AIRPLANES

F-100F

ENGINE	J57-21 OR -21A WITH AFTERBURNER
AC ELECTRICAL POWER SOURCE	ONE ENGINE-DRIVEN AC GENERATOR WITH ONE STAND-BY INVERTER
ARMAMENT	TWO GUNS AND VARIOUS COMBINATIONS OF EXTERNAL LOADS INCLUDING BOMBS, ROCKETS, AND MISSILES (SOME AIRPLANES) MOUNTED ON FORCE EJECTION PYLONS
CAMERAS	SIGHT AND STRIKE
DROP TANKS	TWO 450-GALLON OR TWO 275-GALLON AND/OR COMBINATION OF 200-GALLON
INTERNAL FUEL	FUSELAGE AND WING
REFUELING PROVISIONS	PRESSURE-TYPE (SINGLE-POINT AND AIR REFUELING)
FLAPS	YES, WITH DUCTED FLAPS ON F-100F-20 AIRPLANES
OXYGEN SYSTEM	LIQUID WITH MD-1 REGULATOR
AUTOPILOT	YES

Palm Springs Air Museum F-100D

An ex-Turkish Air Force F-100D in flying condition was acquired and returned to the United States by an American citizen. After flying during the 2004 Reno Air Races, the Hun sat for a little over ten years at the Reno/Stead airport before being acquired by Al Dempsey and donated to the Palm Springs Air Museum where he is a docent. Although the aircraft has not flown in over thirteen years, it is fully functional and is still FAA certified as the only flyable single seat F-100.

After getting an exterior restoration, the aircraft was unveiled at a 6 November 2015 private reception attended by approximately 200 people, 50 of which were former F-100 pilots. The Hun was displayed the following day at a ceremony opened to the public. This only example of a flyable F-100D is now part of the museum's Korean/Vietnam hangar display of aircraft and memorabilia from that era.

(Personal Photo)
F-100D Unveiling Private Reception, 6 November 2015

(Personal Photo)
Palm Springs Air Museum F-100D

(Personal Photo)
Author Adds His Signature to Museum F-100D

(Personal Photo)
Author Gives Approval Getting Into Cockpit After 45 Year Absence.

(Personal Photo)
Okay, Let's Clear All These People Out of Here and Crank This Baby Right Up!

(Personal Photo)

F-100 Pilot Alumni, 7 November 2015

(Personal Photo)

Author With His Two Ladies.

Bibliography

Anderson, David A., North American F-100 Super Sabre, Osprey Publishing Limited. 1987 Print.

Davies, Peter E. & Menard, David W., North American F-100 Super Sabre, Crowood Press Ltd. 2003 Print.

https://en.Wikipedia.org/wiki/North_American_f-100_Super_Sabre, F-100 Super Sabre.

www.defensemedianetwork.com, F-100 Super Sabre Flew Most Missions in Vietnam.

Glenn Tierney, CDR US Navy (Retired), personal interviews and e-mail correspondence, Sidewinder Testing and Development Project.

Printed in Great Britain
by Amazon